COMPANIONING
at a Time *of* Perinatal Loss

Companion Press is dedicated to the education and support of both the bereaved and bereavement caregivers.

We believe that those who companion the bereaved by walking with them as they journey in grief have a wondrous opportunity: to help others embrace and grow through grief—and to lead fuller, more deeply-lived lives themselves because of this important ministry.

Companion
P R E S S

For a complete catalog and
ordering information, write or call:

Companion Press
The Center for Loss and Life Transition
3735 Broken Bow Road
Fort Collins, CO 80526
(970) 226-6050
www.centerforloss.com

COMPANIONING
at a Time of Perinatal Loss

A Guide for Nurses, Physicians, Social Workers,
Chaplains and Other Bedside Caregivers

JANE HEUSTIS, RN. & MARCIA JENKINS, RN
FOREWORD BY ALAN D. WOLFELT, PH.D.

Companion Press is an imprint of the
Center for Loss and Life Transition,
3735 Broken Bow Road, Fort Collins, Colorado 80526

Companion Press books may be purchased in bulk for sales pro-
motions, premiums or fundraisers. Please contact the
publisher at the above address for more information.

Printed in the United States of America

14 13 12 11 10 09 08 07 06 05   5 4 3 2 1

ISBN: 1-879651-47-5

To the loving hands of caregivers
who do make a difference

CONTENTS

FOREWORD

This compassionate book reflects a continuing journey into the art of caregiving to those who experience perinatal loss. As the authors note, "In perinatal loss, families experience a lifetime of change before they ever reach the hospital. In a matter of seconds, the life they dreamed of and hoped for is gone."

Yet, the sad reality is that many parents whose baby dies are greeted with empty clichís:

> *"You're young, you can have other children."*
> *"At least you didn't get to know her."*
> *"You're lucky you never took him home."*

Obviously, these statements discount the profoundness of the loss and create environments in which survivors experience disenfranchisement . They are not accorded the right to openly and honestly mourn.

To be bereaved means "to be torn apart" and "to have special needs." When a newborn dies, parents and other family members and friends come to grief—which is the internal response to loss—and need and deserve to mourn—which is the shared social response to loss. Yet the world that surrounds them often discounts their profound loss.

All too often there is a misconception that because the relationship between a newly born infant and parent is one that is expected to exist predominantly in the future, the bonds that are created during pregnancy are minimal or simply do not exist. In my experience with hundreds of bereaved parents, nothing could be further from the truth! Those persons who do project those attitudes and beliefs are destined to be unresponsive to the needs of the bereaved.

This important book will empower nurses, physicians, social workers, chaplains, and other bedside caregivers to feel good about the care they give during times of perinatal loss. Jane Heustis and Marcia Jenkins have the experience, sensitivity, and vision to write this most valuable resource. They have an authentic and abiding commitment to bring compassionate care and comfort to those families that experience perinatal death.

I had the privilege of meeting these two amazing women several years ago when they attended some of my workshops on the sacred grounds of the Center for Loss and Life Transition in Fort Collins, Colorado. I was immediately drawn to their open hearts and passion for caring for families around perinatal loss. I sensed we would form a lifelong friendship and shared vision of advocating in this vital area of caregiving.

I cannot think of any two people who are more ably equipped to inspire you in this area of grief ministry than Jane and Marcia. Their years of experience shine through in the pages that follow. If your passion in life relates to the care of those who experience perinatal loss, you will want to read and reread this soul-based book. The content will take you on a lovely journey through the application of the companioning tenets and artfully help you make deep and profound connections to those you are honored to walk with and learn from.

I am so proud that this book is anchored in a philosophy of "companioning" (instead of "treating") people in grief. I am deeply humbled and honored that Jane and Marcia have built the foundations of this resource around my tenets of companioning. As you will discover, the companioning model is grounded in a "teach me" perspective. It is about learning from and being totally present to another human being when he or she has been "torn apart" and has "special needs."

I urge you to let Jane and Marcia help you walk with and learn from those families who are willing to be your teachers about perinatal death loss. My hope is that through your capacity to integrate the companioning philosophy into the hospital experience, you as a caregiver will draw closer to and tailor your compassionate care to each families' unique needs.

Thank you, Jane and Marcia, for being the compassionate souls that you are. Thank you for embracing the companioning philosophy of caregiving and providing a framework for practical application at times of perinatal death. And thank you for teaching not only what you've learned about death loss, but about life and living and loving.

Alan D. Wolfelt

PREFACE

"If you build it, they will come."
Field of Dreams

A journey is hard to describe. Its beginning and ending may be formless and fragile, while its middle provides substance and color. Sometimes the path is tentative, other times sure and strong. Fellow travelers heighten the journey, for there is joy in the company.

Marcia and Jane began a journey together 10 years ago as fellow bereavement specialists (despite the fact that we worked at competitive hospitals). We shared highs and lows and offered each other solace and direction in the difficult work of grief care. Three years ago, we connected with Alan Wolfelt at the Center for Loss and Life Transition and learned about his philosophy of *companioning* care for mourners. Companioning fit perfectly in our aftercare programs, but we wondered: could it work at the OB bedside, too?

Our perinatal loss forefathers, the founders of RTS Bereavement Services and Share, developed a new standard of bedside care years ago that has withstood the storms of time. Had it not been for their vision and commitment, OB care during times of perinatal loss would still be in the dark ages—with dead babies whisked away and parents told to move on. Their hard work created a new generation of caregivers that we are fortunate to be a part of. Companioning, for us, feels like a vibrant addition to that time-honored care, another leg in the journey.

As we incorporated companioning into our care, we immediately felt its positive influence and wanted to share the excitement it stirred in us! During animated sessions at the local coffee shop, hours huddled around a computer and long discussions on the phone, we reconfigured Dr. Wolfelt's model for the OB bedside. As writing novices, we weren't sure how to create a book, but we knew that if we could offer a style that fit OB caregivers, others could follow in the journey. If we built it, others would come.

A preface is supposed to explain why the authors wrote the book. Why did we begin this humble journey? As in the movie *Field of Dreams*, a higher power has led us; we do not know what will happen next but we hope you will join us in the journey.

Acknowledging those who have traveled with us

Writing a book is like falling in love for the first time: exciting, confusing, confidence-rattling, heartwarming. Just when the thrill seems over, something happens to cause a buzz once again. It has been wonderful and life-changing.

- A special thanks to Alan Wolfelt, whose life mission is caring for the bereaved. Alan's passion for his work radiated the first time we heard him speak. We are thankful to be a part of his teachings and we appreciate his mentorship. Alan, thank you for believing in us and offering the opportunity to write a book.

- Also thank you to Karla Oceanak, editor of Companion Press. Thank you for your guidance, patience and tolerance. We appreciate your direction when we had no clue where to go. You helped us become writers.

- We would like to acknowledge those people who have come before us, too: Sara Wheeler; Rana Limbo; Sister Jane Marie Lamb; and Cathy Lambert. Without the RTS and Share models of care, there would be no structure to build upon. You did the work when others didn't understand. Your insights continue to lead us.

We also thank our respective hospitals (Marcia's is St. Francis Hospital in Indianapolis; Jane's is Methodist Hospital, Clarian Health in Indianapolis), which have offered us the opportunity to create a career in the world of the bereaved. We are also blessed with coworkers who do the hard work of bereavement care at the bedside. To the ladies and gentlemen of St. Francis and Methodist Maternity Centers, we thank you from the bottom of our hearts. Your energy is in the words of this book.

Most of all, we thank the families whose courage, faith and love has left an everlasting impression on us. Thank you for the privilege of being part of your babyies' lives. This book's mission is dedicated to you.

Marcia's special thank-yous:
My life is enriched by the ones who touch it. I first thank Jack, my husband of 40 years. Without his personal triumph, my dream of nursing would have never come true. His love is and always will be what gives me energy to be the best I can be.

To our son Mike and his wife, Kim, who lost their first child. Sharing that experience opened my eyes and heart to things that fuel me for my work with bereaved families. I hear and remember your words every time I meet a family for the first time. I thank you for our two wonderful grandsons, Kyle and Nick.

To our son Rick and his wife, Carrie, who lost their third child, Jacob. You taught me not to compare grief, for each loss is personal and must be honored. I thank you for our beautiful granddaughters, Katie and Krissy.

To those people I worked with early in my career at Indiana University Medical Center, Dr. John Mackey, Dr. Lillie-Mae Padilla and Gerry Lunsford. Thank you for believing in me before I knew there was anything to believe in.

I owe much to those who companioned and mentored me in my nursing career: the wonderful instructors at University of Indianapolis, especially Dr. Linda Rodebaugh for her guidance in obstetrics; The Sisters of St. Francis and Michelle Wood, RN, for entrusting me with the RTS program; friends Lisa Bauer, RN, and Cher Boys-Fore, RNC, PNNP, who support me daily and commented on the manuscript.

To my dearest and lifelong friend, Connie Edwards, thank you for being there for it all. We have shared so much, even the loss of our grandchildren.

Jane's special thank-yous:
It is said the fingerprints of those who love us leave a lasting impression in our hearts. I thank my mother and sisters, who continue to teach me about bonds that will never fade; my sons, Scott and Tom, whose unending excitement for life fascinates and awes me; my deceased daughters, Becky and Abby, who taught me the meaning of love and courage; and most of all my husband, Ron, who believes in me and encouraged me to write before I even thought I could. Ron, thank you for being my partner in life.

Also thanks to people in my Sunday School class who help me to stretch my limits in faith; my coworkers in OB and Pediatrics who assured me I would never be alone, no matter what the crisis; my coworkers and companions in Women's Services who supply my workplace with energy, insight and friendship; to friends present and past who remind me to have fun and create joy in my life.

To all: thank you for helping me to be what God intends.

Our thanks to each other:
When it is all said and done, the words formatted, the pages printed, the book bound, the best and most lasting part will be the friendship deepened between us. Years ago, we were nicknamed the "Bookends," for we have opposite talents and gifts that balance each other. We hold each other up. It has been a joy producing this book. May this be the beginning of something wonderful in our lives as friends, kindred spirits, and writers. Amen.

INTRODUCTION

*Journey: "a period of traveling; passage or progress
from one stage to another; travel from one place to
another, usually taking a rather long time."*
Random House College Dictionary

A young family walks through the doors of the labor and delivery
unit. Hours ago they were told their unborn baby had died. Aching
with shattered hopes and unfulfilled dreams, this family has
embarked on an unexpected life journey that began with the
unthinkable phrase "I can't find a heartbeat." They have no map
to follow and no trail markers to lead the way.

The next leg of their journey is at the hospital. Here, the staff of
the obstetrics unit has a big job to do. It will be their responsibility
to provide care during the labor, delivery, and postpartum stay.
They will comfort, make mementos, and take photos. They will
offer blessings and suggestions for funeral arrangements. They will
do what they can to make this excruciating experience tolerable
for the family. At the end of the day, they will be exhausted from
the work of bedside bereavement care, for the journey of perinatal
loss changes caregivers, too.

Life and loss in obstetrics

Most people consider obstetrics the place where life begins, but an
estimated 2-4 percent of hospital delivery rates end in loss. In fact,
many OB units have losses equal to their hospital's adult intensive
care units. We know that adults die of complications in illness or
injury, but babies? Babies aren't supposed to die.

In labor and delivery, families with drastically different outcomes
share the same hall. Staff members alternate the masks of comedy
and tragedy as joyous births unfold next door to tragic deaths. A
nurse may place a brand new baby still wet from delivery into the
arms of a mother among cries of celebration; hours later, she may
offer a stillborn baby into the reluctant arms of a mother who

doesn't know what else to do but cry. A chaplain may go from blessing the beginning of a life to asking God to comfort a grieving parent. A doctor changes hats as he first tells a patient that she is going to be a mother then informs a family down the hall that their plans for parenthood are over. The work is overwhelming and conflicting.

It is often assumed that pregnancy and birth are rites of passage and will happen as planned. Families affected by perinatal loss often say they knew someone who had a pregnancy loss but never considered it would happen to them. It is unfathomable in our society that a parent would survive her own child, because in this age of excellent medical care, people only die when they are old, after they have lived their lives. Many families in their childbearing years report little personal experience with death. Some never have seen the inside of a funeral home.

In other areas of the hospital, death is the ending to the hospital stay, but in OB, families often come to the hospital knowing their baby has died or is going to die; for them, grief begins on admission. The initial hours and days of crisis happen while they are in the hospital, not at home. Grief support isn't a matter of assisting the family in viewing the body or helping make calls. Away from their usual support systems, families need intense TLC and grief care. Caregivers must provide physical care to the mother while offering bereavement support to the many family members who may stay around the clock. Caregivers find themselves intensely providing care for mother, father, grandmother, grandfather and siblings, while trying to manage deliveries and care for other patients. OB bereavement care seems impossible to accomplish at times.

Obstetrics caregivers are pivotal characters in the story of loss. Families come to the OB unit in total shock, unsure how to proceed. Long into the future, their story reflects the quality of their hospital experience. How they chose to mourn and cope with their loss in the months and years following the death was definitely impacted by the in-hospital care they received. Some families report leaving the hospital with mixed feelings. Did they have a baby? Others will relate how their caregivers showed them the way and gave them permission to grieve over a tiny baby whom the rest of society may not acknowledge. Caregivers such as nurses, doctors, midwives, chaplains, social workers, and unit support staff touch the patient and family and create an environment for healing. Their care sets the stage for future mourning.

It's all about caring

Why are healthcare professionals drawn to obstetrics? Perhaps it is the adrenaline rush of birth, the passion of hands-on support or the thrill of watching new families begin. We are instruments of caring and we love what we do. Our business is babies—healthy, vibrant ones who will join loving families and live happily ever after. It's easy to forget that not all babies survive.

Many of us struggle to provide bereavement support. Our compassionate side wants to reach out to the family but we feel unprepared and unequipped. Most hospitals offer a standard of care for perinatal loss patients, but few provide staff education and training to ensure that standard. Contributing to our unease, perinatal loss happens infrequently enough to lessen skills. Depending on the number of deliveries, a unit can go weeks or even months without a perinatal loss patient.

Most of all, perinatal loss doesn't feel "right" because it goes against the grain of what we are taught about the outcome of prenatal care: that is, if a mother seeks early care, follows her provider's instructions, and delivers in a controlled setting, her baby will be healthy. A death of a baby seems so different than what we experience most of the time. It is uncomfortable and some of us tend to avoid those patients when we can.

On the other hand, some of us are drawn to bereavement care. We have a passion for the work and volunteer whenever the perinatal loss families come to our unit. We may have had a pregnancy loss ourselves or cared for a patient who touched us in a way that could not be forgotten. We know they need us, yet the work is still emotionally exhausting and draining.

Whether we shy away from or are drawn to bereavement patients, we agree: watching them suffer is overwhelming. It is our nature to want to make it better and alleviate their pain. We try to soften the blow by paternalistically making decisions for them. We work to push them through the labor curve, do their postpartum teaching, and put them "back on track," but their pain does not go away; it becomes a wall that seems impossible to overcome. We depend on technology to tell us what to do rather than relying on our instincts. We even resist the emotionality of grief, which can affect the patient's response to medications and impair communication. Our efforts, well intended, usually fail.

Our unit procedures and protocols, which are our usual landmarks and guides, don't always fit bereavement situations. Like dominos, when one piece fails to meet the patient's needs, whole systems fall apart. We know we must break down barriers for the sake of the patient and family and find better ways to care for our bereavement patients. We need ideas and strategies; we need a road map for the journey.

Creating a new model

Companioning can help us draw the road map we've been searching for and give us a new perspective for bedside bereavement care.

What is companioning? It isn't a magical formula or an A-B-C guideline. It is more a framework, an attitude, a presence. It is a shifting of philosophy; we no longer will view perinatal loss patients as needing treatment or intervention. Rather, we will see their loss as a life-changing event, one that is an intensive part of our OB culture. Our care evolves away from protocols and standards and towards family-directed care. The roots of the word companioning are the basis to the philosophy: "com" means "with" and "pan" means "bread." A companion is someone you would share a meal with. A friend. An equal.

Companioning helps us better see what families need to get through the deaths of their babies while giving us permission to be the compassionate souls we hope to be. As companions, we let go of preconceptions and begin to see grief as a natural event. We start to honor grief as it happens and when it happens, letting families mourn as they need to, despite traditional schedules. Companioning helps us to see ourselves as guides rather than rescuers. We have skills and experience but our willingness to be a part of the experience will have the biggest impact.

Dr. Wolfelt coined his philosophy *companioning* after many years of working with the bereaved and seeing the lack of understanding in society. He knew that people needed to be lifted up in their grief and allowed to suspend until they were ready to embrace their pain. They needed companions to witness their grief, not discourage it. Adding companioning theory to the hospital experience will help us as caregivers to draw closer and tailor care to each family's specific needs.

How can companioning help?

Marcia: I first heard Alan speak at a conference in Indianapolis. As he explained his vision for companioning, I quickly realized that it was the missing piece in my care of patients and families. His words painted a picture of a personal journey of loss, with a path that led to beginnings and endings, as a grieving person found new directions. The path was also dotted with darkness and light, with the changing landscape of emotion. He talked about a sacred place where those traveling in the pain of loss could suspend until they were ready to move on. He helped me see that I was privileged to walk alongside, to be present as doors opened that allowed families to embrace their grief. Alan's paraphrase of Helen Keller's powerful words—"The only way to other side is through"—stuck with me and made so much sense. As a caregiver, I wasn't responsible for making them better. I was only responsible to be a partner in the process.

Jane: Marcia told me about Alan's ideas of companioning. Just listening, I knew she was right: companioning was the missing link in my practice, too. I began to revise my intentions as I worked with patients. I no longer felt the burden of needing to be in charge, having to handle it all. I went into each room wanting to explore the meaning in their story and I let my interventions naturally flow. I found I did a better job in meeting their immediate needs and felt more connected in the process. When I finally heard Alan speak in 2001, I knew I was on the right track. Companioning would help me do the kind of work I wanted to do.

Companioning encourages the evolution of our traditional way of thinking and helps us explore the personal challenges we face in bereavement care. It empowers us to go the extra mile in ways that are healing for family and staff:

- We realize we don't have to do "the whole thing." As professionals, we are the experts in the physical components of the mother's labor, delivery, and postpartum, but when it comes to grief care, the family knows what is best for them. Companioning relieves the caregiver's burden of trying to predict and time care; instead, the family leads the way.

- We don't have to worry about "saying the wrong thing." In companioning, quiet presence and silence are as valuable as words. Communication is based on the family's need, not on the caregiver's plan or agenda.

- The raw emotion of the situation does not have to be a roadblock. Companioning teaches us to witness and honor the pain of loss. We let go of our own issues and see the family's pain as a part of the healing process.

- We don't have to feel like outsiders in a foreign place. Companioning helps us to be curious, ask questions, and help build a life-remembering experience.

The companioning concept draws a picture of a compassionate caregiver and provides a guide in maneuvering the wilderness of grief and loss. Although it may seem hard to grasp at first, companioning is formed by our own natural instincts as caregivers. It is who we hope to be.

ALAN WOLFELT'S
TENETS OF COMPANIONING THE BEREAVED

Companioning is about honoring the spirit; it is not about focusing on intellect.

Companioning is about curiosity; it is not about expertise.

Companioning is about learning from others; it is not about teaching.

Companioning is about walking alongside; it is not about leading or being led.

Companioning is about being still; it is not about frantic movement forward.

Companioning is about discovering the gifts of sacred silence; it is not about filling every painful moment with talk.

Companioning is about listening with the heart; it is not about analyzing with the head.

Companioning is about bearing witness to the struggles of others; it is not about judging or directing those struggles.

Companioning is about being present to another person's pain; it is not about taking away or relieving the pain.

Companioning is about respecting disorder and confusion; it is not about imposing order and logic.

Companioning is about going to the wilderness of the soul with another human being; it is not about thinking you are responsible for finding the way out.

Beginning your own journey

We invite you to begin a new journey with us and experience perinatal loss from a companioning perspective. We want to provide tools for your journey and ways to feel good about the kind of care you offer.

We encourage you to let the following real-life stories of co-workers and families touch you. We hope you can let go of fears and insecurities, gain some practical skills and learn to use your intuitive caring. Most of all, we hope this book will help you see yourself as a companion, one who is willing to "walk alongside" as you open yourself to an experience you will never forget.

Come journey with us into the world of perinatal loss, where, sadly, babies die, but families and staff can have the experience of a lifetime.

CHAPTER ONE

FAMILIES: BECOMING PART *of* THEIR STORY

John and Mindy experienced the stillbirth of their first baby at 40 weeks gestation. This is their story, told at a support meeting months later.

They arrived at the hospital early on Monday morning. Contracting since the evening before, they showed up in triage—video camera rolling—ready to greet Matthew, their soon-to-be-born son.

Both were so excited they didn't notice the nurse's difficulty finding the fetal heart rate. After a few tries, the nurse announced she was going to get an ultrasound. They weren't even thinking about anything going wrong. The doctor had had trouble a few times in the office because of Mindy's larger size. When the resident doctor, a person they had never met before, spoke the words "I can't find a heartbeat," Mindy said, "Can't find it? Where did it go?" As soon as she said it, she saw a look of horror on John's face. The doctor continued, "I'm sorry, Mrs. Harris, but your baby has died."

Mindy thought: this isn't possible; the baby was moving just this morning. Besides, she had done everything her doctor asked and read every book on pregnancy. She asked for another doctor. When a second doctor verified the diagnosis, she asked for another ultrasound machine. Not until Mindy's own doctor came did she begin to believe. John sat by the bedside dumbfounded, unable to speak. Mindy thought about crying but couldn't. Rather she felt someone had lifted her up and put her someplace else. She knew she was in the bed and she saw people talking but couldn't hear what they were saying. John experienced the opposite: it was as if the walls of the cubicle closed in, trapping him, forcing him to hear every word. Thoughts of losing his wife as well as his son raced through this mind.

Mindy was quickly moved to a labor room. An IV was started and epidural placed. Staff talked to her about seeing the baby at delivery, but their words were garbled to her. John stood nearby, not sure what to do. When the chaplain suggested he contact family, John mechanically made calls, telling them "there might be something wrong with the baby." He couldn't make the "real words come out."

Matthew was born about 12 hours later. They decided to wait to hold him. Mindy said she was too exhausted from the delivery and John agreed. Looking back, they realize they both were too afraid—afraid of what he would look like, afraid of what his lifeless body would feel like, and, most of all, afraid the pain would be too overwhelming. It was their nurse who helped them overcome their fears. She called Matthew by name and referred to him as their son. She also gave them a Polaroid picture taken after he was dressed. Mindy said, "He looked so sweet in that picture, my heart just melted."

John and Mindy took turns holding him. John would close his eyes and pretend Matthew was still alive. He even read him a book he brought to the hospital called Love You Forever. Staff came in and out of the room, providing care and comfort, but neither John nor Mindy remember much about that. They just remember Matthew.

Matthew's little body appeared perfect and there was no apparent cause for the stillbirth in the cord or placenta. When they asked about the peeling of his skin, they were told he had probably been "dead inside for one or two days." Despite her fogginess, Mindy heard that comment. "He died on Saturday evening or Sunday morning?" she asked. Mindy immediately reviewed everything that happened in the two days prior to delivery, wondering what she had done wrong. She was afraid to ask questions, especially with John in the room. She thought he would blame her for the death of their baby. Not until months later did she realize that John was going through the same process, blaming himself.

Their doctor told them he didn't know why their baby died and suggested an autopsy. "What will they do?" John asked. The doctor explained they would examine Matthew's body, looking for birth defects or complications. "How will they do that?" Mindy asked. The doctor explained it would be like a surgery. "They will cut on his body?" Mindy interjected. Mindy decided that no one was going to cut on her baby. He had been hurt enough. Despite further encouragement from the doctor, no autopsy was done.

Matthew stayed in their room until Mindy was ready to go home. "It was so hard to leave him behind," they both said. "I felt so empty, so hollow. When we were at the hospital, I felt Matthew was still a part of me. Once we left, without Matthew and without all the people who went through it with us, I felt I had nothing left. I wasn't the same person anymore."

Mindy remembers the shock wearing off about a week later. She woke up one day and "it hit her like a ton of bricks." She couldn't stop thinking about how it happened. Did she do something on Saturday night? Was there something that she should have noticed, some sign that should *have alerted her to possible trouble? Could she have prevented his death? She searched the internet and joined chat rooms. She checked out every book in the public library on stillbirth. At her postpartum checkup, John and Mindy asked her obstetrician, who could only say that "for most stillborn babies, we never know why." They both felt that not knowing why was almost as painful as the death itself.*

When asked if there was anything that the hospital staff did that was helpful (or not helpful), they both said: "Everyone was so wonderful. There was this one nurse. We couldn't have made it without her. She talked to Matthew and sang to him as she gave him a bath. Gosh, we probably would have never even seen him without her. The thought of that scares us—not ever seeing him. We owe her everything."

In perinatal loss, families experience a lifetime of change before they ever reach the hospital. In a matter of seconds, the life they dreamed of and hoped for is gone. No one would argue the intensity of their pain, but do we truly understand it? We have a mental picture of what families go through and an expectation of how they should react, but is it accurate?

To companion families, we must see loss from their point of view. As caregivers, we cannot step inside their shoes and feel what they are feeling, but we can become curious, enter into their story and honor their need to grieve as they choose.

When there is no baby to parent

All parents create a mental vision of their unborn child: He will be a baseball player or she will be a dancer. He will be an honors student or she the first woman president. He will look like his daddy;

she will have red hair. Once the baby is born, each parent must let go of the wished-for child and bond with the here-and-now child. Their baby may not look or act the way they thought, but they love him or her just the same. The transition happens quickly and seamlessly; most parents aren't even aware that they are letting go of one while they are embracing another. From the first second their baby is put in their arms, a new and wonderful relationship begins.

When a baby dies, there is no baby to continue the relationship. Like a road that abruptly ends, there is nowhere else to go. It is said that when a loved one dies, the people left behind are suspended between the past that they long for and a future they were only hoping for. For them, life comes to a standstill, for nothing forward makes any sense or meaning. As one mother put it, "It's like sitting in a waiting room for eternity, waiting for what you expect, but nothing ever comes." For John and Mindy, the news that their baby died caused a total standstill. The rest of the world appeared to speed by yet they weren't sure where to travel next. They were stuck in the chasm of loss; they couldn't go forward as planned but certainly could not go back to their pre-delivery state. For families like John and Mindy, the present world feels empty and the past is only shattered hopes and fading memories. Perinatal grief is about the loss of hopes and dreams and the actual death of a baby. Parents grieve over the loss of both.

In a single moment, life as they knew it ends. They experience emotions they have never felt before, ones that have no names in their current vocabulary. When John heard the news about his unborn son, he stood helplessly by, unable to move, make plans or calls. The word "bereaved" literally means "to be torn apart." Each parent has his or her own reaction to bad news, but all feel torn apart from the experience they expected, the one that included a new baby to tend and love. John and Mindy came to the hospital expecting a healthy baby and a new family. They got neither. Hearing the words "there is no heartbeat" tore them away from everything that was familiar, predictable and safe.

Each family bonds with their unborn and begins a relationship that is seeded in love. When the baby dies, the intensity of that love causes feelings of emptiness and loss. There is no doubt that perinatal loss families love their babies, but there are times when fear can temporarily override those feelings. John and Mindy were initially afraid to experience their dead baby after delivery. Some of their fear probably stemmed from society's general discomfort with death, but much was caused by being forced to enter a new and foreign world—the world of grief. Fear can be temporarily more powerful than love and can paralyze families at first. They need someone to help the fear fall away so they can love their baby at this crucial moment. John and Mindy were fortunate to have such a person caring for them after delivery.

The unique and personal side to grief

Like a fingerprint, grief is a one-of-a-kind experience, unique to each person. Each member of the family experiences the same loss but may focus on different elements and/or outwardly express it in his or her own way. John and Mindy appeared to be traveling down the same path after the loss of their first baby, yet John withdrew when in pain while Mindy questioned. Ordinarily, John was the decision-maker in the family, but during crisis, he was unable to fulfill that task. (John told the support group later that he wasn't sure why and was disappointed in himself about that.)

Family members—mother, father, siblings, grandparents and friends—each create a mental image of their relationship with the baby-to-be; that vision will shape their unique response to the loss. Cindy and Dan, another couple who delivered a non-viable baby, had different reactions from the very beginning. Cindy was more focused on her inability to carry a child to term (this was her second loss), while Dan was more preoccupied with the fact that this baby was their first male child. (It was a rite of passage in Dan's family to hand down the family name to the firstborn male.) Cindy cocooned after the delivery, talking about future pregnancies rather than spending time with her son; she needed to address this important piece before she could approach her feelings about her baby. Dan and Cindy also had a five-year old daughter named Hannah. When she came to the hospital to visit, she avoided the baby, clinging to her grandmother or playing with the bed controls instead. Hannah seemed more focused on the emotional changes of her family than her deceased sibling. For Hannah, the fact that her mommy and daddy had changed caused a loss for her.

Parents experience other losses along with the death of their baby. They must face the loss of their status as parents, something that is highly valued in most cultures. Without a child in their home, they will not be seen as parents. The mother may have a caesarean scar to prove her motherhood, but if the crib is empty, she is not a "mother." Significant relationships are affected, too. Many parents report changes in their feelings about their partner because of the loss. Some say the shared loss made the relationship stronger, but some report the opposite. Jillian, a mother who lost her baby at 20 weeks, told the chaplain at a memorial service, "We were engaged to be married but then the baby died and we realized that all we had together was grief and that wasn't enough. I felt like he was always bringing me down. I had to get away." Parents also report changes with friendships, especially those who have children or have never have experienced a loss. "They just don't get it," one mother said at support group. "They think they are better than me." Previous relationships and friendships fail, making the emptiness and isolation even more prominent and hurtful.

Parents can teach us about grief

When we open our minds and hearts, parents can teach us about grief and its effects. The following are some of their messages:

Grief is personal. Mindy and John demonstrated classic signs of crisis: shock, disorientation, denial, and confusion. Not all families grieve that typical way. Parents may display uncontrollable emotions or they may be stoic and distant. They may be distracted or act as if nothing has happened. Trisha, a young mother who delivered a baby with unknown birth defects, played cards and joked with friends just hours after her baby died. When the social worker asked how she was doing, she replied, "I have had bad things happen to me all my life, what's one more? Do I wish she was still alive? Heck yes, but what does that have to do with anything?" Atypical grief responses don't mean they didn't love their baby.

PERINATAL LOSS:
WHAT DO FAMILIES GRIEVE FOR?

- A baby, the one they planned for
- Changes in the predicted family make-up, one less member of their family
- An opportunity to be a parent
- Change in relationships between partners: Each parent will grieve differently
- Opportunities for future pregnancies and children
- Level of self-esteem: "I'm not the person I thought I was"
- Status in social circles: Do they "belong" among friends who have children?
- Financial worries: Grief temporarily impedes ability to work
- Physical changes: "I don't feel like the person I used to be"
- Feelings about the future in general
- Sense of security and control in life
- Hopes and dreams: For this pregnancy and for life in general

Not all grief follows a textbook. Family members cope in ways
that are right for them at the time.

Grief is not in proportion to the size of the person. John and Mindy's
baby was 8 pounds and 15 ounces, a good size for a full-term baby,
but in the total scheme of life, Matthew was not a proportional
member of society. He was a tiny baby who never made it home
from the hospital, never took his first steps, went on a first date or
attended college. He was big enough to wear newborn clothes but
not "important enough" to warrant an official birth certificate or
social security number. His mom and dad had prepared nine
whole months for his coming—a lifetime to them. Even families
that deliver a very early baby have similar feelings. Tessa and
Emilio had been trying to have a baby for over eight years; when
they delivered their twins at 17 weeks gestation, they grieved and
mourned over their tiny 8 ounce bodies as if they were grown children. To them, they were; after all, they have been hoping for and
dreaming of the twins for almost a decade.

The numbing of crisis is powerful. The shock of their initial experience impairs the families' ability to think, express themselves and
make decisions. They report being in a fog or feeling fuzzy. Time
seems distorted and things move in a slow, freefall manner, waiting for the mind to catch up. Their hearing is tin-like and it is difficult to process the words. Mindy reported she knew people were
talking but couldn't "hear" them. Everything feels urgent but nothing gets completed. This period of numbness is the body's way of
isolating itself from the stress of the experience. It is like a failsafe
or a surge protector, shutting the system down when the energy
level gets too high. The person is protected from the intense and
raw pain of loss but at a price: they cannot receive or give information. They may not be able to explain what is important in their
need for support. Months after delivery, a mother told her midwife
that she was surprised at how she handled the death of her baby.
"I'm usually so assertive," she said. "I ask for what I need. But I
just lay there and let everyone make decisions for me. It was like
my mouth didn't work."

Pain is part of the experience. Parents teach us about the pain—the horrible, soul-eating pain that follows the death of a baby. The pain is more than emotional; it is also physical and spiritual. Some is relieved by the support of those around them, but most lingers. Kind-hearted, well-meaning caregivers try to take away the pain, but their efforts are often superficial. Kerry remembers the nurse who tried to divert her attention by talking about an actor on TV; she remembers thinking, "Who cares? My baby died and I don't care about things like that anymore." Donisha, whose physician ordered morphine IV push just prior to delivery in response to her intense screaming, has only vague memories of the delivery, baby's bath and baptism. "They stole it all away," she said. "The only time I had and they stole it all away." Donisha's caregivers were only trying to help to ease her pain; they didn't realize that they were adding to her misery. Paternalism—making decisions on the parents' behalf—seems the only recourse when families cannot express their wishes. Still, the pain is there and doesn't go away. It is hard for us to understand that pain must be part of the experience, for it is the pain of love. If they loved their baby, then they will hurt when he or she dies.

Compounded pain and grief can become too much to bear. This is especially true for parents who have experienced other recent losses in their lives, such as divorce or separation from loved ones. They may have had other deaths in their lives or maybe this was a multiple gestation pregnancy with the loss of more than one child. Other losses can temporarily impair their ability to mourn, for grief comes at a time when they are totally depleted and unable to feel any more pain. For these families, grieving will have to be delayed. Patty was a mother of a premature baby who died in the NICU. Patty's mother had died soon after she found she was pregnant and Patty was still mourning her mother's death when she went into preterm labor. After weeks in the hospital, she delivered a micro-preemie who "had nothing but problems from the get-go." When her daughter, Lacie, died, she secretly felt relieved. She needed to "get away from it all" for awhile. The impact of her daughter's death did not really hit her until Lacie's birthday a year later.

What is important

What is important to families during the initial stages of grief?
Weeks and months later, when asked the simple question "What
helped you most while you were in the hospital?", families usually
report the following:

- *"They treated me like I was special but not a freak."* Many parents
  struggle with the fact that they are different that the rest of the
  patients. They failed to do what everyone else in the world
  seems to be able to do (i.e. have a healthy baby). Parents appreciate being treated with respect and dignity, not as "different
  than the rest." They appreciated those who honored their
  temporary state and viewed them as capable people.

- *"They let me take my time and never pushed. They helped me
  make decisions but let me make them."* Parents receive a lot of
  advice, especially from well-meaning family members and
  friends. They easily get overloaded with options. They need
  informed caregivers who watch for clues of readiness and gently
  introduce subjects. They need guidance in making decisions
  such as seeing the baby, but don't need someone to make decisions for them.

- *"They thought of everything I never would have, like taking
  pictures or having my best friend come to see the baby. My baby's
  little memory box is my most prized possession."* Parents appreciate those caregivers who focused on creating positive memories, thinking ahead when they couldn't, and concentrating on
  details for them.

- *"I think my nurse loved my baby almost as much as I did. She
  talked to him and held him, and cried when he was baptized."*
  Parents remember caregivers who were willing to be part of
  their baby's life and provided value to their experience.
  Caregivers who demonstrated those behaviors were role models
  for mourning, too.

- *"When we first got there, we wanted them to hurry and get the
  baby delivered. I wanted them to put me out and do a C-section.*

I'm so glad they didn't; I wouldn't have been ready if we had done it so quickly." Even though they initially want to rush through the experience, parents appreciated those who encouraged them to slow down in order to make life-impacting decisions and collect life-lasting memories.

Finding their story

There are many pieces to the family's story we will never know. Once families arrive on the unit, time constraints and the numbness of crisis challenge their ability to relay their story. Yet, the story is what fuels our care, begins trusting relationships and creates the foundation of the journey. Their story is what helps us define the darkness in their wilderness. As we care for perinatal loss patients, we must look for ways to find the hidden parts of their stories so we can individualize their care and provide light in the midst of darkness.

We may not truly understand what it is like to lose a baby, but we can enter their story and allow the family to show us what is important. It is our mission and our privilege.

THE POWER OF A STORY

We all have a story. Our story paints a picture of what has happened and marks a particular point of view. Each time the story is told, it is pulled from our memory, where it has been safely stored.

With each story, we invite another into our life: listen to me, see as I see, feel what I feel, share with me, know me. In telling the story, we find meaning and purpose. The telling makes it more real.

The listener has a part in the story, too. As we listen, we begin a new path with another person. Their essence imprints on our memory and we begin to feel them within our hearts. Their story teaches us about what is important and prepares us for similar circumstances down the road.

A story changes and renews us. A story is part of the journey.

CHAPTER TWO

CAREGIVERS: ENTERING INTO *the* WILDERNESS

This is a story about a delivery of a pre-viable baby through the eyes of three caregivers: a nurse, a doctor, and a chaplain.

Tasha had been admitted earlier in the week for labor at 21 weeks gestation. In the early hours of Wednesday morning, her membranes ruptured, so medications were discontinued. Tasha and her fiancé, Jayson, were told to prepare for imminent delivery.

When nurse Melissa arrived on the unit that morning, she scanned the board and saw her name next to Tasha's. She sighed; bereavement was the last thing she wanted to do that day. The off-going nurse reported that Tasha's contractions were every three minutes with heavy bleeding. "It won't be long now," the nurse said. "I tried to talk to them about what will happen, but she's too out of it and I don't think Jayson gets it yet." The night nurse worried that Tasha and Jayson had not grasped that their baby was going to die. As Melissa walked towards Tasha's room, her neck and shoulders tightened. She didn't know what it was like to lose a baby. She had two healthy kids at home and she "wasn't up to all the sadness" today. Why me, she said to herself, then immediately felt guilty about considering her own discomfort rather than Tasha's.

Dr. Brown was the resident physician for the day. Three nights ago, he informed the patient that the odds of continuing the pregnancy were slim. He had suggested they "let nature take its course," but Tasha was adamant they try to save her baby. He knew the future of this pregnancy—weeks of bed rest and medications. Tasha, 19 years old, was a student at the community college. Her schooling and life would have to be put on hold. The most she could hope for was staying pregnant long enough to

deliver a micro-preemie destined for long-term problems.
Dr. Brown had wondered if he was allowing her to make
the right decision. Now he stood at the end of Tasha's bed.
Better this ends now, he thought. Not knowing what else
to say, he squeezed her foot and left the room.

Dan was the on-call chaplain for the day. He had a
congregation on the south side and filled in at the
hospital when needed. Dan never minded visits to labor
and delivery; his wife, Cindy, was pregnant for the first
time and he was very excited about becoming a dad. He
didn't find out why he was called until he got to the unit.
He wanted to tell them no, I don't know anything about
babies who die. His chest got heavy and he wanted to cry.
Bible in hand, he went to see Tasha and Jayson anyway
and offered them prayers of hope. Maybe it won't turn out
the way the nurse said, he thought. Since it wouldn't be
long, he decided to wait in the staff lounge.

At 7:45 a.m., Jayson ran down the hall yelling, "Something
is coming out!" Melissa followed him into the room and
saw Tasha's panicky face. "There's something between my
legs!" she cried. Before Melissa could even pull back the
covers, Tasha choked out, "Please God, no."

Tears of helplessness formed in Melissa's eyes. Her
instincts told her to go find help; she didn't want to do
this alone. She couldn't remember the last time she delivered a tiny baby like this one. But she knew she had to
stay. If she left, even for a minute, Tasha's panic would
escalate. She took a deep breath and told herself, "Get your
butt in gear, get the warmer on, the cart open, call the
doctor. Get this over with."

Melissa tried to make eye contact with Tasha because she hadn't really introduced herself. Tasha looked at her and said, "Is my baby here?" Melissa gently pulled back the sheet and saw that Tasha had delivered. She touched Tasha's arm and nodded. "I need to call Dr. Brown. Are you OK for a moment?" She looked at Tasha, then Jayson. They both nodded and Melissa went to the intercom. She still felt panicky but tried not to show it. She laid out the softest blanket she could find and moved toward the bed. She waited until Tasha looked up at her then said, "Is it OK if I go ahead?" Tasha was beginning to shake all over. Although she didn't want to, Melissa went ahead and cut the cord.

When he got the call, Dr. Brown thought about the unfairness of why this happened to such nice people. He dreaded finishing this delivery. Something about a woman crying got to him. In the room, the lights were turned down and he could hardly see. Tasha wasn't draped like his usual patients. Dr. Brown liked routine, but he figured he'd have to adapt his typical procedure. He walked to the bedside, pulled on gloves, and silently completed the delivery of the placenta. Unsure what to do next, he stood quietly at the end of the bed and watched the nurse introduce their baby. He saw Jayson move closer and touch the baby's arm. Jayson, a husky football type, was crying. Dr. Brown felt a lump in his throat and "swallowed until it went away." He moved around the bed, put his hand on Jayson's back and looked at the baby, too. He could see pulsating of the cord and movement of the arms. He wanted to check the placenta and estimate the blood loss but he waited. He knew, despite his discomfort, this was a moment not to be disturbed.

As Dan waited to be called, he thought about what words he could offer that would make this situation better. He was usually a positive man, but what could be positive about this? Tasha had requested a baptism immediately after birth. Dan's denomination didn't believe in baptism of babies; they viewed it as an act of salvation, reserved for those who could make a choice. He thought about their request and remembered how important their faith was to them. He finally decided this baptism could simply be an act of sacred prayer they needed for healing. About 15 minutes after delivery, he was called back to the room. Hands trembling, Dan performed the baptism on Eli Josiah, a tiny little child of God. He carefully filled out the baptismal card and handed it to Jayson. As the family circled in prayer, he felt a peace in the room he hadn't felt a few hours ago. For the first time, Dan was glad he came.

Tiny Eli Josiah lived about 30 minutes, cradled in his parents' arms. Throughout the day, Melissa, Dr. Brown, and Dan offered physical, emotional, and spiritual care to this new family. Mementos were gathered, paperwork filled out, and postpartum teaching completed. When given the choice, Tasha opted to spend the night. Extended family and friends came and met Eli, too.

Melissa was exhausted at the end of her shift. She figured she would cry all the way home, but as she changed out of her scrubs, tears didn't come. She couldn't get Tasha's look of panic out of her mind, but as she chatted with her co-workers in the locker room, the memory slowly transformed to one of Tasha caressing her tiny son. It had surprised her how both Tasha and Jayson had looked so happy with this baby who was too small to live. There's a lesson there, she told herself.

Dr. Brown delivered 5 more babies throughout the day, one right after another, giving him little time to think about it all. "All in a day's work," he was heard saying at the end of the day. That night he treated his kids to pizza and video games.

Dan went back to the church to sort out how he felt about infant death. "It was an overwhelming experience for me. I did a lot of praying that day." He decided not to share his day with his wife, at least for awhile.

All three said it was a day they will never forget.

Families look to caregivers to produce what they have hoped for—a new baby. The OB unit becomes the conduit of their dreams, the final leg of the pregnancy journey. In the eyes of patients and family, we are the magicians who make it all happen.

When a pregnancy ends or a baby dies, we no longer hold miracles in our hands; we now carry shrouds of pain and disappointment. Our task becomes helping the family say hello and goodbye to their tiny baby. These are big shoes to fill. Melissa, Dr. Brown, and Dan knew that watching a baby come into this world too small to sustain life is one of the hardest scenarios OB personnel have to encounter.

For many of us, this new role seems beyond our grasp. We wonder if our lack of experience, both professional and personal, makes us less effective caregivers. We worry our current skills won't match the situation. We think we don't know how to care for a family experiencing a loss. We search for training and instructions. We figure that with enough job aids we can care for these families, but we are wrong. What we need are ways to feel good about bereavement care. We need to be able to say, at the end of the day, we made a difference.

The art of companioning can paint a new picture of our role as bereavement caregivers. Companioning can take us from traditional methods that weigh us down to new ones that lift us up, helping us offer the kind of care families need. Becoming a companion is essential for our survival in a world where miracles are not to be.

Learning about ourselves as caregivers

What is our "job" as caregivers? We care for the patient and her family throughout the labor, delivery, and postpartum experience. We provide support. We are the ones who "get them through." We may have to skip a meal or stay over, but we get the work done. We say we do it so patients get the care they deserve. We do it for us, too: something about helping a family in dire need fuels us.

When the loss of a baby is added to the situation, everything seems to get turned upside down. Getting the family "through it" takes on a whole new meaning, for both the family *and* the caregivers. Melissa, Dr. Brown, and Dan didn't want to travel to the forest of grief that day. It felt dark and awkward but they knew they could not walk away.

The first step in overcoming our discomfort and embracing the journey of grief is to shed old beliefs and notions about our role as bereavement caregivers. Like layers of heavy clothes, they bog us down, weigh on our confidences and isolate us from real issues that challenge and direct us. Each caregiver must come to the conclusion that:

• *We, too, grieve when a baby dies.* We mourn over babies who shouldn't have to die. We fill with emotion as we work with families. Feelings like sadness, confusion, anger, and guilt are natural for caregivers. We are afraid—afraid to enter into the family's grief, afraid of how we will feel, afraid we won't be able to handle it. It is hard to enter into another person's crisis when we are filled with personal emotion. Grief work is hard for caregivers.

• *Sometimes our only choice is to come to the family empty-handed.* We are out of our comfort zone when a baby dies. We are unsure and don't trust our instincts. Dan, the chaplain, worried that his current knowledge and experiences weren't enough. He had to stretch his comfort zone in order to reach out to Tasha and Jayson.

- *Our assumptions about grief and loss desensitize us.* Reactions to loss are intensely personal and unique. Even if we have had a personal experience with death, we still don't know what it is like for this family. We don't know how we would react until we have truly walked in their actual shoes. We can make general predictions of what families might need based on previous experiences, but we will only know what this family needs when we ask. Lynda, an OB support worker, had a baby who lived in the NICU for six weeks before she died; Lynda knows firsthand the heartbreak of losing a child, but she is quick to tell parents that she only knows how grief was for her. In her words, "I am a kindred spirit, someone who has walked a similar walk. That doesn't mean I am more of an expert than the next guy." It is common to hear "If that was me, I would..." or "I wouldn't feel that way about..." The fact is we just don't know how we would feel in the same situation. *The only people who know how they feel are them.*

- *There are some things we just can't fix.* We can't take away the pain, we can't bring the baby back, and we can't change who they are—their coping mechanisms, current support systems, family dynamics, etc. All of us can think of a time we wanted desperately to make it better for a patient but couldn't. Melissa, the nurse in the story, said later the hardest part of taking care of Tasha was not being able to make it better, no matter what she did. Watching them struggle through each new task reminded her of that. It wasn't until she saw them begin to grasp the death of their baby and cope that she felt she could relax. We must come to the conclusion that it isn't ours to fix.

When we discard these burdens, we might feel empty at first. What else is there to depend on? When we dig deeper, we find a core of caring that brought us to our profession in the first place— a wanting to help others and a willingness to be there. After all, that is all families really ask of us: to help them in areas they can't help themselves.

Different roles, different gifts

As bedside caregivers from different disciplines, we each play a
unique role in companioning grieving parents.

Doctor—The doctor often establishes a relationship with the
patient prior to the loss and is the most likely member of the team
to provide consistency in the long haul of grief. As the bearers of
bad news, the planners of care, the holders of loss post-discharge,
doctors often carry the heaviest burden, too. Patients often expect
their physician to be professional but personal at the same time—a
difficult combination. Many physicians have little training in the
world of death and often feel uncomfortable in loss situations.
Even when there was nothing that could have been predicted or
prevented, they often feel a sense of responsibility. As they try to
sort through their own feelings, they must keep going because
there are many other patients who need care.

Midwife—Midwives bring excitement and empowerment to the
journey of pregnancy. When a complication such as fetal death
occurs, their low-risk scope of practice is challenged. Depending
on the delivering facility and practice, some midwives continue
with the patient, while others may have to sign the labor and delivery portion over to a medical doctor. At a time when the patient
and family need their midwife the most, different caregivers may
step in, leaving both the midwife and the patient feeling a loss of
the hoped-for delivery as well as the loss of the baby. Midwives
continue to support the patient and family in the weeks and
months following the delivery. Depending on the patient's risk fac-
tors, they may even see the patient for a subsequent pregnancy.

Chaplain—Chaplains often come to the bedside with little medical
background or preparation. They must overlook things that are foreign to them and be open to the moment, even if it is personally
uncomfortable. They bring wholeness to the grief support team,
offering the unique and vital element of faith and a kind of comfort
that goes beyond medications or treatments. Sometimes, families
look to a chaplain or pastor for specific direction and/or answers
to the "why" questions. The chaplain must stay centered and meet
the family on their faith terms, even if it means moving temporarily

out of their faith zone. Their ability to listen when needed is their greatest gift, along with their words of prayer and solace.

Social Worker—In the world of bereavement support, the role of the social worker varies from one institution to another. In some hospitals, social work is an active member of the team, while in others it is a resource for staff. Social workers bring a wealth of knowledge regarding community resources to the team. Moreover, the family sees them as someone they can talk to about personal/psychosocial issues. Their quiet presence and willingness to listen is evident at the bedside. They are also knowledgeable about how to help with other life stresses (such as financial concerns, family support, etc.). Social workers broaden support beyond traditional bereavement care.

Nurses and Nursing Staff—Nurses care for the patient as individuals and as a collective unit. They provide hands-on, intimate care 24 hours a day. Together they embrace the totality of care as they care for physical, emotional and spiritual reactions of grief. Often, they become the "gatekeepers," alerting and organizing the other members of the team. They also must embrace the physical aspects of death, such as handling the baby's dead body, dealing with death protocols, etc. Their greatest gift to the bereavement experience is being present and available.

Working toward companioning

Whatever your specific role as bedside caregiver, there are eight essential concepts to consider when preparing to be a companion. Each one helps overcome the stigmas that prevent us from drawing closer and finding more comfort in the darkness. Some are easier said than done; many need practice to achieve.

1. *Let go of the old stuff.* Throw out previous notions about perinatal loss and grief and start anew with each family. Think of each new bereavement situation as a clean canvas: the family is the artist and you hold the supplies.

2. *Explore your own fears and emotions.* What are the hardest parts for you personally? How do you feel when you are with these

patients? Sometimes acknowledging these feelings helps put them into perspective. Seek out support people, such as coworkers, other team members or supervisors, with whom you can talk about your feelings.

3. *Separate your responsibilities for the physical care from your participation in the grief care.* There are many facets of care that we as professionals must provide and some grief-related care that we can just let flow. For example, consider which kinds of pain you can work to relieve and which kinds of pain are part of healing.

4. *Let the family be in charge of their own grief.* You do not have to direct or manage grief. Use care plans as guides rather than schedules so the family can pace the intensity and timing of care.

5. *Practice "being still."* In companioning, it is essential to have periods of inactivity and quiet. In the hospital, being still doesn't mean not moving. It means working at a pace that is soothing and non-stressful instead. It also means that sometimes there is nothing to be done. It's OK just to be with the family, without performing specific tasks. As you practice being still, become more aware of the power of your non-verbal presence and the message your body language is giving.

6. *Rely on your intuitive caring rather than your skills.* Sometimes you will have to leave your expertise at the door and replace it with your natural curiosity—an attitude that says "tell me more, I'd like to know." It may take a while to get used to the idea that skills are not the first line in assessment. Most professionals know what it means to listen to your gut. The challenge comes in trusting that instinct.

7. *Redefine what is meant by a positive outcome.* If a healthy baby is the only acceptable outcome, then every time you care for a bereavement family, you will fail. If you can't change the outcome of the baby, what can you change? You can offer the best day they can possibly have. Frame your thinking to the present: what can I do right now, in this moment, to help?

8. *Prepare yourself for the exhausting work ahead, physically, emotionally and spiritually.* When you're caring for a bereave-

ment patient, take rest breaks when you can and drink lots of fluids to avoid the achy muscles of dehydration. Think about how emotions affect your body and watch for signs of personal overload. Create support systems to get you through, both in the hospital and out. Most of all, believe in yourself. You can do this work and you will make a difference.

As we work towards companioning at the bedside, we spend more time with the family. We become energized with their story and we see areas where our care and guidance is a positive influence. We begin to feel good about what we do in these scenarios previously defined as "hopeless."

Companioning helps us to develop a new outlook

We see honor in the spirit of grieving families. We believe they are capable of entering into grief and surviving. They will survive without us, but we have the opportunity for participating and enriching the experience.

We become curious about what is happening with the family in their grief and want to know more about what it is like for them. We want to ask; we want to know.

We begin to learn from each family about their unique grief, which helps us to focus on what is right for them. They will give us the information and timing, and we will create the care map.

We start to walk alongside, to be a part of their special experience, offering support and guidance. We find it easier to walk alongside rather than accept the burden of carrying them.

We practice being still because we see that the family doesn't need frantic movement forward. We practice patience because it needs to be about them.

We discover how sacred and helpful silence can be, especially in moments when words don't work. We let other things demonstrate our caring.

We realize we can also listen with our hearts instead of always using our heads. We can let go of traditions and textbooks, practicing with the core caring that brought us to the profession instead.

We work towards accepting and bearing witness to the family's struggles without judging or intervening. We see that struggling is part of healing.

We become present to the family's pain, for we realize we cannot take it away. We will comfort and ease their journey as we are able, but we acknowledge they will still be in pain. Their pain partners with their love and we would never want to take that away.

We can function within the disorder and confusion because we see that order and logic won't help the situation at this time. What seems chaotic to us may be OK for the family.

Most of all, we are willing to go to the wilderness of the soul with the family without feeling like we are responsible for finding the way out. We are the companion and guide.

The next step

Companioning can be challenging. Some bedside caregivers will still feel lost and search for a quick tip-sheet. Companioning is a matter of changing perspective and attitude. It doesn't just change our practice, it changes us.

Once we become familiar with companioning, we begin to see our care in a new light. We rethink our previous notions and reformat our thinking. When we admit a family, how will we change our approach? How will we talk to families as we explain options? Will it change time spent at the bedside? These are questions (along with many others) we must continue to explore when converting to companioning.

What is the next step? Enter into the wilderness and begin.

CHAPTER THREE

ENVIRONMENT: CREATING *a* SPACE *for* MOURNING

This is a story about a woman who taught us that a simple labor room can become a sacred place.

Candy found out her baby was going to be stillborn on her third prenatal visit. This was her fifth baby—not exactly planned, but her first child with Billy. They had been together for about two years and hadn't expected to get pregnant because Candy had had her tubes tied after her last delivery. She didn't suspect her symptoms as signs of pregnancy until well into her fourth month. Both were giddy with excitement about this baby. They had already purchased many baby items, including a crib they found at a local thrift shop. Both "fell apart" when they heard the baby died.

From the first visit, Candy had secretly worried about the baby. Before finding out she was pregnant, she was "doing bad stuff for a baby," such as smoking and drinking occasional beers. The doctor had been very kind as she told Candy the news and assured her that she hadn't done anything to cause the death of her baby. Still, Candy blamed herself.

On the day Candy was scheduled for induction, she woke early, drank four cups of coffee and smoked half a pack of cigarettes. She was hyper and restless by the time Billy pushed her out the door. At the last minute, she put a baby blanket and stuffed Pooh Bear into the bag they had bought to take to the hospital before all this happened.

Shellie was the nurse assigned to admit Candy. With the limited information on the induction schedule—a G5P4 26 week IUFD— she went to prepare Room 14 for Candy's arrival. She pulled back the covers, laid out Kleenex, and pulled the curtain around the baby cubicle. She thought the warmer would be too painful for them to see, since there wouldn't be a baby to put there after delivery.

Mary, the bereavement support nurse, checked in with Shellie as she laid out the rest of the supplies. They talked about the pros and cons of pulling the curtain. Mary thought that "it looked like we are hiding something." Shellie thought "it was cruel to make them look at it." They both saw each other's point of view and weren't sure what the best course would be. Mary suggested a compromise: She removed the resuscitation equipment and draped the warmer with a soft bath blanket. She added color—a pink and blue blanket and a tiny teddy bear. She turned on the dimmer lights to give a glow to the area and rotated the warmer so it faced the bed. She pulled the curtains slightly.

The visitor's aid greeted Candy and Billy with a smile and words of encouragement. "Let's get you to your room. I know you have a long day ahead. Shellie is going to be your nurse and she'll take good care of you." Candy refused to lie on the bed, picking a chair in the corner instead. Billy knelt down beside her.

Before Shellie could introduce herself, Candy blurted out, "What's behind that curtain?" Startled, she said, "The baby warmer." Candy rose from her chair and asked, "Where will my baby go since you got that shut off?" Mary had followed Shellie into the room, heard the question and tried to help. "Candy, my name is Mary. I am one of the support nurses here. Would you like for your baby to be in the area we traditionally use for babies or would you like a special crib so your baby can be closer to your bed? Either is OK with us—whatever feels right to you." Without saying anything, Candy pulled out the blanket and Pooh Bear and walked across the room. She pulled the curtain and laid her blanket over the bunny one. She tenderly put Pooh in the corner and removed the bear Mary had placed there only minutes before. "We won't need this; we brought our own," she said. "What do we gotta do now?" were the next words from Candy's mouth.

Shellie and Mary spent the next hour trying to help make Candy comfortable with the environment. Candy refused to change her clothes, so Shellie put a gown in the bathroom and told her she could change when she was ready. Candy asked very frank questions like "What does a dead baby look like?" and "If my smoking killed her, will we be able to tell?" When all questions were answered, Shellie began the standard admission procedure. After papers were signed, room orientation done and forms completed, Shellie was ready to alert the resident doctor for orders. However, just as she was leaving the room, she looked over and saw Billy sobbing. Mary had pulled a chair next to the bed for him to be close to Candy, but during the last part of the admission, he must have slipped back to the corner. Candy got up and with IV pole in hand, comforted Billy.

Candy's induction officially started four hours after her arrival on the unit. Her labor went quickly and she delivered six hours later: William Arnold Dinkins Junior, "Junior" for short. Both Candy and Billy bathed and dressed him and kept him in the room until she was discharged.

*Hours later, Candy figured out how to detach the
bassinette from the warmer and pulled it closer to her bed.
She laid out each of his mementos—footprint cards, angel
pin, baby ring, etc.—in the bassinette, encircling him. She
also put a rose Billy bought in the gift shop and the
sympathy card her mom had brought. The nurse helped
them take four rolls of photos, many of Junior lying among
"his things." It was a precious site, a sacred place for a
special baby.*

Hospitals may be places of respite and healing, but their environments are hard on the senses. The feel of an OB unit or NICU is one of hustle and bustle, noise and movement. This can be intimidating to a family in crisis, especially when they are already having trouble hearing, seeing, and feeling. Patients and families can be overwhelmed before they arrive on the unit. Depending on the size of the hospital, just coming from the parking garage, past the lobby, through admitting, and up the elevator can be exhausting.

The atmosphere of the hospital sets a lasting impression for families. There are some parts of a hospital environment we cannot change, but there are many areas we can. Even the smallest changes can promote a companioning environment, one that invites both families and staff to participate in the emotional and spiritual work of grief.

A companioning environment

The philosophy of companioning can transform the environment of an obstetrics unit to one of openness and healing. A companioning environment:

• *Creates a feeling of safety for the family*. It is a place of security and comfort, one that says you are welcome here, no matter what you are experiencing.

• *Accepts and encourages grieving and mourning* and creates an honorable, sacred place for the baby. Death is a normal part of life and reactions to loss can be openly expressed.

• *Provides an empowering environment for caregivers,* one that helps connect with families without distractions or pressures.

Companioning environments lift up and enhance the companioning tenets of honoring the spirit, maintaining curiosity, and listening with the heart. Stillness, silence, and presence flow. The new environment opens avenues for sharing and learning from each other. It also minimizes distractions that might deter the work of mourning. Families have a hard enough time confronting the death of their baby; they don't need added roadblocks. Candy taught the staff that family-perceived negative environments can quickly escalate issues. She hadn't been in the room five minutes before she felt uncomfortable. She also saw an environment that did not honor her baby, her prized possession. If Candy's caregivers hadn't been able to adapt the environment, she and Billy wouldn't have been able to fully experience the birth and death of their baby in the way they wanted.

Preparing the environment for companioning

A carefully prepared environment will help families embrace the pain of loss and concentrate on making positive memories. A companioning environment:

Is soft and unobtrusive. Low lighting, pastel colors and subtle textures create a look that is easy on the senses compared to the starkness of most hospital rooms. The noise level and amount of movement nearby are important, too; families need to be in a space where outside distractions are at a minimum. Softening the environment acknowledges the family's need for simplicity at a time when little things can quickly overload them. According to Candy, just seeing the "big white bed and the Kleenex" threw her into a whole new state. "All I could see was a big white feeling of pain. I didn't even want to go near it."

Acknowledges the family as a unit. The room and unit should accommodate the whole family, not just the patient. There should be a chair next to the bed for the partner and plenty of seating for other family. Ideally, the unit should also have a designated place nearby for extended family to wait other than the standard waiting room. A grandmother awaiting the birth of her first grandchild, who would likely die after delivery, told a charge nurse, "Do you have any idea what it is like in that waiting room? It's all balloons and happiness. I'm not going in there."

There should be a special place in the room for baby, too—one that says he or she belongs there. This concept can be controversial. Is it more hurtful for families to see the baby area or is it more hurtful to have it hidden from view? In a companioning environment, we prepare for both, for it is the family's decision. We may need to spend time exploring the concept with them, but in the end they choose. If we adapt the current space, we create a space of honor that demonstrates how special we think their baby is. It took Mary a few minutes to remove obtrusive equipment and drape the warmer, but what a difference it made. The curtain could have remained pulled throughout the admission if that had been Billy and Candy's choice, but Mary's thoughtful preparation offered them alternatives.

Is open, accepting and dependable. Environment is more than walls and furniture. People impact environment, too. In order to create an accepting atmosphere, all staff must be on the same page. Each caregiver who could potentially interact with the family should know of the loss. Units often use verbal reports, assignment boards, etc. to relay family info. Some hospitals use markers on doors to alert staff. Everyone from housekeepers to medical directors needs to be unified in bereavement care. The last thing a family needs is for some well-meaning person to congratulate them on their new birth. All staff should call the family by name with each encounter and offer their willingness to help. A dad asked a support group leader, "Who was on the other end of the intercom? That voice was one of the kindest people we met and we never even met him!" Another mom said, "Even if our nurse wasn't available, my husband could always find someone to help. We couldn't believe how nice they all were." When staff work together to create an aura of helpfulness, families never feel alone.

Family has choices in how the environment will be healing for them.
For many hospitals, there are few choices as to where the mother will labor/deliver, but there are policies within the unit that can be adapted. Does she have to go to a recovery room after her C-section? Can she stay in the labor and delivery room for postpartum? Can she have more than the allotted visitors? In companioning, we first explore what would be healing to a particular family, then adjust the environment, as much as we can, to fit their needs. As we work towards a healing environment, areas become sacred; that is, a part of the room becomes full of honor and love. The dictionary defines sacred as "reverently dedicated to some person or object." The bassinette was a sacred place for Candy and Billy. Candy started by placing items she brought to make it personal for her baby. Later, she even moved it to the middle of the room and created a display of Junior's precious things. The bassinette contained the total life of their lifeless baby, the only place her baby ever "lived." Candy's caseworker understood. She commented about its beauty and asked permission to look and touch the items. "It was kind of like a shrine," she said after visiting "A shrine to somebody she loved more than anything in the whole world."

Doing an environment check

It's hard for caregivers to see the unit as parents see it. To us, it looks the same each day because we have learned to be comfortable in the space. How can we see what needs to be done to improve the environment for grieving parents? Going through the following checklist will help:

For the unit:
• *The front desk and/or triage area*: Do all staff know of the situation so they can greet the family accordingly? Is the process from desk to room timely so the family doesn't have to wait for long? (Even two or three minutes can be eons for a family who has just received bad news.)

- *Alternative waiting area:* Is there an area near the patient's room that is ready for family members if they cannot go immediately to the room with the patient? Are there comfort items such as phone, drinks, pillows, etc. available to them? Do they know they can go back and forth as needed to the patient's room?

- *The hallways*: Are hallways free from extra equipment and beds, especially immediately outside of the room? Is staff minimizing noise near the room?

For the room:
- *Room choice*: Is it a room that dulls the noise of the unit, perhaps one that is off the main corridor or near a side entrance? Is it away from patients who are actively laboring, if possible?

- *Room set-up*: Is excess equipment and clutter removed? Is there seating for family, especially within touching distance of patient?

- *Color*: Are there splashes of colors among the hospital white—tones easy to the eye such as mauve, light green, light blue, cream? Pink or blue in the baby area?

- *Lighting*: Are the overhead and/or fluorescent lights off, using indirect lighting or natural sunlight instead? (The room should not be dark.)

- *Bathroom*: Are there personal hygiene supplies set out so the patient won't have to ask? Bath supplies for partner, too?

- *Sleeping accommodations for family:* Are there pillows and blankets laid out on admission so they can get comfortable when they are ready?

- *Baby area:* Is unnecessary equipment removed or out of sight? Is the look of the warmer or bassinette softened with soft blankets, adding color and/or stuffed animals, creating a card with the baby's name (if known before delivery)?

- *Chair for staff:* Is there a chair for staff to use when in the room so they can be at sitting level when talking to families? (Rolling procedural stools are great for this task.)

When thinking about environment, remember that little things mean a lot. Gestures as simple as having a pitcher of ice water and cups in the room and tissues on the nightstand say a lot about our willingness to provide comfort. Families may not notice the changes staff make to the environment for their sake; they'll only know that their room feels safe, secure, and comforting—a place where they can begin the work of mourning.

CHAPTER FOUR

COMMUNICATION: BEGINNING *the* CONVERSATION

This is a story about Kelly and her nurse, Debbie, who was there when Kelly needed her.

Kelly was a single mom in her third pregnancy. A routine ultrasound showed massive hydrocephalus, incompatible with life. At 29 weeks gestation, Kelly decided to have the pregnancy induced because the baby's head was nearing full-term size.

During admission, Kelly spoke frankly and openly about her baby's diagnosis and her decision to induce the pregnancy. Her mother, father, and fiancé, Tim, came with her and were very supportive. The unit staff remarked how well she was doing, how "together" she was. Yet two days later, Kelly was still not laboring despite four different induction agents. The doctor told her she had two options: cancel the induction or have a surgical procedure. Kelly was devastated by the news.

When Debbie, one of the L&D nurses, heard the update, it touched her heart. She had met Kelly soon after admission while covering for a coworker and was surprised the induction hadn't worked. She wondered if something else was going on. She talked with the doctor and together they decided to continue the induction until 7 pm.

Debbie found Kelly disheveled and exhausted, staring at the TV. She didn't even look up when Debbie walked into the room. Lights were off and the room was cold. Family members were spread over the room, anxiously watching Kelly. In response to her mom's question, "When will we know if they have to do surgery?" Kelly buried her face in her pillow. Debbie was curious about what Kelly was thinking, so she asked if they could talk together. The family, hearing the request, offered to get some dinner.

Debbie sat close to the bedside, turned up the lights a little so she could focus on Kelly's face and changed the TV to a music channel. "I feel for you, Kelly," she began. "You've been through so much." They sat in silence for a few minutes. Debbie patiently waited, concentrating on her facial and body language. She wanted Kelly to know she had her full attention. When Kelly looked at her, Debbie said, "What do you think is going on?" Kelly finally said, "My baby won't come." Debbie sensed a need to be closer and touched Kelly's arm.

Kelly began to cry. "I'm afraid it will be like last time," she sobbed. Debbie had heard that one of Kelly's babies had been adopted out but didn't know anything else. She asked, "What happened last time?" Kelly told her about making the adoption decision, then the labor ending in C-section for fetal distress. "It all happened so quickly. As soon as I delivered, everything was out of control. My whole world just sped by." She didn't see or hold that baby (a decision she made during the pregnancy). She didn't regret giving up the baby but the whole process was full of emotion and pain. "I'm not sure I can go through that again," she said. She connected the Cesarean section with the whole ordeal and felt the surgery had complicated her recovery when she "needed to move on."

Debbie slowly moved the conversation to this pregnancy. When she asked Kelly to explain how she felt about this baby, Kelly told the story of falling in love, getting pregnant, then finding out that her baby "would either die or be a vegetable." Tim had named her Chelsea early in the pregnancy and they had been calling her that since. Kelly and Tim had talked about Chelsea suffering both before and after birth; that was the main reason they decided to go ahead with the induction. Kelly was torn between "doing what's best" and "getting it over with." Debbie waited for a pause in the story to confirm what she heard: Kelly loved this baby and wanted only the best for her. She wanted to see and hold her baby, a part she missed the last time.

Mothers in similar situations had taught Debbie that induction medicines don't work if a mom is not mentally ready to experience the death of her child. She softly and carefully explained this to Kelly, encouraging her to "let go" temporarily of the past and concentrate on the present. She explained the importance of allowing her body to do the work of labor. Debbie offered Kelly the opportunity to have the very best day she could have with her baby. Kelly pronounced, "I think I'm ready, if you'll help me."

Debbie assisted Kelly into the shower, letting the warm water soothe her aching muscles. She repeatedly reminded Kelly to "relax and let your body do the work." She also referred to Chelsea by name and reminded her she would be here soon. She wanted Kelly to be focused on the part that would encourage her—seeing and holding her baby. She involved Tim, too, showing him how to massage Kelly's back during contractions and support her labor. The family began to follow Debbie's actions, speaking quietly and slowly to Kelly in affirming words. Three hours later, Kelly's cervix was 5-6 centimeters dilated. By 8 p.m., Kelly was ready to deliver.

Baby Chelsea was born at 8:36 p.m. and died in her mother's arms about two hours later. Debbie was by Kelly's side despite the fact her shift had ended three hours before. Kelly's parents were there, too, sharing in the moment. Kelly and Tim's pastor visited and offered prayers and blessings for the tiny baby prior to her death.

The next day, Debbie went to visit Kelly on the postpartum unit. Kelly asked, "How did you get me to deliver?" Debbie replied, "I just helped you do what you needed to do." Both began to cry and hugged each other for a long time. Kelly asked for a picture of Debbie holding Chelsea. Debbie was glad to honor the request.

Months later, the support nurse and Debbie talked at length about Kelly's delivery and how Debbie felt about it. When asked which part had impressed her most, Debbie replied, "Watching her explore her own story, find the hard parts and let them go." Did this experience change Debbie? "Absolutely! How can I be a part of something like that and not be changed? I feel so fortunate to have been able to help her. Sure, some of it was my skills, but most of it really was because I was in rhythm with her. That's all she needed. That—and time."

Communication is *the* most important skill we have as healthcare professionals. Along with our eyes and hands, we depend on our ears for information. Whether it is the lub-dub from a stethoscope or an interview with a patient, our ears take in the data we need to process what is happening.

When it comes to perinatal loss patients and families, communication is our biggest fear. We are afraid of the silence, so we fill empty spaces with words—or we are afraid to say anything, so we limit our time in the room. We're not sure how to use skills that in other circumstances come naturally. How can we companion families when we are afraid to talk to them?

Communication and crisis

Crisis is second nature in OB: whether it is a precipitous delivery, emergency section or a hemorrhaging patient, we must work quickly and efficiently. Adrenaline surges as our heart rate soars and sweat forms on our brows; our bodies prepare for the work of crisis but forget to include our mouth and ears. It's hard to communicate in a crisis.

Families have trouble communicating in a crisis, too. It is said that a person only hears about 20 percent of what is said in a crisis situation. When parents receive devastating news, they are thrown into a tailspin of shock. They remember only bits and pieces of conversations and fragments of important information needed for decision-making. No wonder perinatal loss parents appear confused and misinformed; they have heard less than a quarter of what is said.

In a crisis, families often communicate with people they have never met before. Because there is no prior relationship, they focus on the person rather than the message. They expend their limited energy evaluating trust and miss content in the process. We continue to talk but they don't hear us. Everyone gets confused.

The crisis path of the family's journey creates a dilemma: we need to give them vital information, but they can't hear us. Stop by any nurses' station and hear: "I already talked to them about that. Did they say no one had?" Initial crisis stresses us all.

The essence of communication

In the hospital, we focus on facts and figures; our communication is give and take, report and documentation. In the previous story,

Kelly's caregivers thought they knew all about her because they had read her prenatal records, scanned the genetics consults and asked the standard admission questions. Their assessment pronounced she was doing well in her grief. They forgot to consider that there might be more to the story.

Communication isn't just "tell me what I want to know and I will tell you what you need to know." It is more than giving and receiving. In its purest sense, communication is:

- An opportunity for expression, to state what is on our mind.
- A process of clarifying thoughts, making sense.
- A way to seek acceptance, as others react to what we are saying.
- A re-energizing—because being heard gives us a reason to continue.

Communication becomes the tool with which we enter in and understand. When Debbie heard the doctor talking about Kelly, she was curious and wanted to know more. When she listened to Kelly, she learned vital pieces to the story. Debbie gave Kelly the opportunity to explore her own story, put names to emotions and find perspective. She offered Kelly a beautiful gift: the opportunity to be heard and understood.

In companioning, the essence of communication is placed in the hands of the family. Their ability to communicate may be like a swollen river, blocked with rocks and debris. Our job is to help them remove the obstacles that hinder its flow; we help them communicate with us. We listen instead of always talking; we honor silence as well as words. We learn to hear with our hearts as well as our ears. Communication becomes a conversation of caring, a "help me understand" attitude.

Entering into a caring conversation

> *Conversation: "A communication between two persons; a mental connection."*
> Random House College Dictionary

When we participate in conversation, we come together for a short time as partners at a table of trust and acceptance. We join because we want to know, not because we have some information to tell. A conversation is not "let me explain about options for care," it is a "tell me what you are thinking about" forum. Instead of looking at communication as a tool for dispensing information, it becomes the method for linking pieces of information together to form a chain of connection.

Creating conversations of caring is a matter of removing obstacles so words and thoughts can flow:

- *Clear your agenda to allow the time the family needs.* When Debbie wanted to focus solely on Kelly and her family, she asked the charge nurse to reassign the rest of her patients for the next four hours.

- *Prepare the room for listening.* Think about potential distractions like lights and noise. Turn off cell phones and mute pagers. Debbie lowered the TV volume and limited the people in the room so both she and Kelly could listen.

- *Be aware of your physical presentation.* You don't want to become part of the distraction; remove scrub jackets or jewelry if needed. Sit at their level. Relax your shoulders and lean forward slightly. Focus on the patient or family member's face. Let your appearance give the message you are ready to listen.

- *Create a circle of intimacy.* Who should be a part of the circle? Kelly's family voluntarily left when Debbie asked to talk, but many parents feel more comfortable when significant others are close by. It is important to ask the parents, "I'd like to talk about what's going on. Whom would you like to help in that conversation?" A circle of intimacy is also physical. Make sure chairs are arranged in a way to limit movement when speaking. If not, your attempts to include others in conversation who are sitting outside the circle will be distracting to the mother. A space within three feet (touching distance) of family creates closeness and encourages the ability to hear.

- *Open with an introduction.* Offer your name and state your function and/or purpose in simple language. For example: "My name is Judy and I am one of the chaplains at the hospital. Dr. Johnson told me what was happening and asked me to stop by." Or: "I am Cindy and I'll be your nurse for the next eight hours."

- *Add an expression of empathy to convey additional messages.* Let them know you know what is happening (so they don't have to explain it to you) and you want to help. You might say, for example, "My name is Kristi and I'm the nurse who will get you settled in. I was sorry to hear what happened to your baby." Or, "I'm Mrs. Sanders, the social worker for labor and delivery. I heard you got some difficult news today." Empathy does not have to always be expressed in words; body language will also demonstrate a caring attitude. Georgia, a labor and delivery nurse, feels that words of empathy sound hollow when the person is a stranger. She works at showing them, instead, with touch. Statements of empathy, in words or gestures, need to be genuine and uniquely yours.

- *Wait until they are ready to listen.* It is respectful to wait until you have the family's attention. Approach the bed, sit near the bedside (if possible) and wait until the mother or family acknowledges your presence. The nurse in the story provided an excellent example. She patiently waited until Kelly mentally came to her before asking any questions. If she had begun before Kelly was ready, the ensuing discussion might not have happened.

- *Be curious.* It is OK to ask questions, especially when they are asked in a frame of "tell me more, I'd like to know." Examples of opening questions might be: "Can you tell me what happened today?" "What is going on right now?" "What is the hardest part for you right now?" Avoid questions that can be answered with a simple yes or no when possible.

- *Restate and/or clarify parents' thoughts to assure understanding.* Debbie let Kelly do most of the talking, speaking only to rephrase Kelly's thoughts or ask a question about something that wasn't clear. Debbie's restatement of Kelly's words—"All the things you've told me said that you really love your baby and want what is best for her. Is that right?"—gave Kelly permission to explore a new avenue. Restatement and clarification helps the speaker as well as the listener.

- *Honor silence and non-verbal messages.* The family is moving at a much slower pace than the staff. Silence is a way they can try to catch up in the conversation. It is also a great time to focus on non-verbal behaviors—messages they are sending when words can't explain.

- *Offer openers, if needed, to help the conversation get started.* The general rule is to listen more than talk, but that might be diffi-cult during initial contacts, especially when families demon-strate an inability to express thoughts. Examples: "Sometimes it is helpful to talk about..."; "Tell me what's weighing on you right now"; or "Other families in this situation often talk about..."

- *Tell them about others.* If a family has trouble getting started, stories of previous families may help. Start by saying, "Many families in your situation tell us... is it that way for you?" It is vital that this technique not be used to categorize or pigeonhole families; it is only meant to get the family started. "Yes, I feel that way, too" or "No, that is not what it is like for me" begins the conversation. Talking about other grieving families also provides a normalcy at a time that feels utterly abnormal. Ginny, a mother who delivered a baby with Turner Syndrome and hydrops, asked, "Did any other mothers with a baby like mine hold their babies?" Ginny needed to know that others had doubts, too.

Offering information

Families need direction to make good decisions. They need us to outline what is possible, yet the information is often overwhelming and confusing. Our goal is to present information in its clearest and most helpful way:

- *Concentrate on present issues first.* Let the family's requests, demonstrated in their words and non-verbal cues, start the process.

- *Offer one concept at a time.* Information needs to be repeated multiple times, using the same language, until the family is able to absorb it. A respectful way to frame the repetition might be, "I want to talk to you about your choices for getting your labor started. I know this is an overwhelming time and your brain feels a little fuzzy, so we'll talk for awhile, then I'll come back in an hour and we'll go over it again."

- *Use your voice as a tool.* The tone of your voice will often affect their ability to hear and concentrate. When offering information or discussing options, speak in a lower voice, slow your speech and pause every few sentences.

- *Use family-comfortable words when possible.* We often forget that healthcare providers have a language all our own. Families often get lost trying to understand medical terms during conversations. Even words that seem simple to us can sound foreign to families. A well-educated mother told her grief support caregiver a year after her loss, "When the nurses said the word 'bereavement,' I didn't know what they were talking about. It sounded so harsh and ugly. It's kind of silly that I didn't get it, but at the time I didn't even want to ask." When possible, use terminology that family uses first.

Conversation and culture

The word "culture" can elicit a unique response from every caregiver, for it is often defined as those things that seem "different" than us. Culture is more than language, race, religion, or ethnicity.

FAMILY-COMFORTABLE LANGUAGE: ALTERNATIVES FOR MEDICAL WORDS

NICU	newborn intensive care
Bereavement	grief; pain of loss
Dead	lifeless
Missed abortion or products of conception	miscarriage
IUFD, fetal death	died before birth
Induction	getting labor started
Sloughing or maceration	fragile skin
In caul	baby still in the bag
Placenta	afterbirth
Pathology, Autopsy	tests after death
Shroud	special wrapping
Morgue	special waiting place
Burial	committed to the earth

Culture is also molded by socioeconomic status, family origin, folk beliefs and practices, ethical positions, biases and prejudices, and chosen lifestyle. How the family chooses to interpret life events and express their grief is all a part of the culture. In other words, a person may look, dress and talk like you but not share the same culture. For example, all families that speak Spanish do not have the same culture; their country of origin, family makeup, level of education, and amount of acculturation will affect expression of their heritage. A family may be Caucasian, attend the Methodist church, and have kids in the hospital daycare, but they may also be a same-gender couple—a culture all its own.

The art of companioning is especially important when entering into another's culture. Curiosity and learning from others becomes premium despite its challenge. How can we connect with people whose culture may be different than ours?

- *Listen and observe the family.* Their interactions may tell you about the essence of their culture: the role of men and women, generational authority, level of language skills, personal space and touch, etc. When Lisa spoke to a family from Kenya about burial arrangements, she watched the father and saw that he was the spokesman when it came to death issues. The mother turned away every time the word "baby" was mentioned. She ordinarily did not exclude the mother from conversations, so she asked, "Is talking about your baby's burial something your wife wants be a part of?" The father's answer was, "She is not allowed."

- *Ask to assure you understand.* Each family carries it own unique expression of their culture. At a local hospital, two families from Mainland China experienced the stillbirth of their babies in the same week. The first couple declined to see the baby, refused all mementos, and said that it was their culture "to forget." When the second family arrived two days later, the staff made some initial assumptions about what this family might want, but they were wrong; the second family spent long periods with their baby, asked for family photos, and were grateful for the Memory Keeper. It's OK to ask: "I don't know much about..." or "Tell me what's important..."

- *Always offer a translator when English is the second language.*
Even for families that speak English well, crisis may affect their
ability to think in a non-native language or there may be medical
concepts that need translation. Families can always decline the
offer of translation, but they will know it's available when
needed. Sonya, a young mother from Vietnam, lost her baby at
22 weeks. She was able to converse in English and no translator
was called. Four days after discharge, the home visit nurse
found Sonya had massive engorgement. She had been applying
heat and massage to ease her breast pain. When the nurse asked
her if engorgement had been discussed in the hospital, she
remembered the word but didn't know what it meant. Also, her
postpartum instructions were only in English; no one asked her
if she could read English.

- *Assure that the translator is comfortable in discussions about birth
and death when translation must be used in conversation.*
Translators often become interpreters, too. That is, certain
concepts cannot be literally translated because of cultural
issues. Also, translators—even native speakers—may not know
how to best translate sensitive issues. George, well versed in
Spanish, was asked to help a chaplain talk with a family. As the
family talked, George began frowning and fidgeting in his chair.
He said to the chaplain, "They're asking about incineration.
What are we talking about?" George's non-verbal cues caused
increased discomfort for the family. Later, George told the chaplain, "I've never had a conversation like that." Translators must
be part of the caring team, more than "repeat what I say."

Continuing the conversation

Since patient and family stay in the hospital for many days, conversation becomes a continuous motion, one that flows from family to caregiver, caregiver to caregiver, and caregiver to family. With
each conversation, links are added to the chain, lengthening and
strengthening it. It is like a boat that continues down the river,
picking up passengers and cargo along its journey. Each conversation enriches the process.

Some caregivers will be a consistent voice in the conversation, seeing the family multiple times during the hospital stay. Others may only spend a shift or have one short encounter. All have a vital role in continuing the conversation. Our job is to create a seamless system where families feel the connection of conversation rather than fragments of multiple ones:

• Reintroduce yourself with each encounter and remind them of your connection: "I'm Sally; I met you earlier, in triage."

• When possible, introduce caregivers who will follow: "This is Judy, your nurse for the next few hours. She and I have talked about everything that has happened so far. She will take good care of you."

• Recap previous conversations to continue the flow: "Yesterday we talked about ..." or "Dr. Smith talked to you last night about..."

• Work as a team to learn the whole story. A story often comes together like pieces in a jigsaw puzzle. The grandmother may relay things to the nurse while the mother is talking to the housekeeper mopping the room. The chaplain or social worker may hear parts of the story that family feels are too intimidating or embarrassing to discuss with the doctor. Sharing elements of the story will reveal deeper meaning.

• Share the story with others. It is important to relay the story to other caregivers on the unit so they understand. The unit secretary may not have an opportunity for unlimited discussion with a family member, but they do field calls and direct visitors. They need to know what is important to the family, too.

Your willingness to hear their story and ask questions tells the family that you are ready to enter into their grief. It can create a cycle of caring. The more you know, the more personalized care you offer, the more they tell you, the more care you are capable of providing, and so on. The process elevates the bar as you become a part of the continuing story as their companion.

PARENTS SEARCHING FOR INFORMATION: SAMPLE CONVERSATIONS

Why did this happen?
"We don't know why this happened to your baby. Many parents worry that they did something to cause it; for some that is the hardest part. We will try to find answers if we can. We can do tests on your baby after he dies that might give some answers. For some babies, we may never know why they died."

Do I have to...go through labor, see the baby, have a funeral, etc.?
"There are some things that can't be changed, like when a baby has to be buried, or how you deliver your baby, but we'll try to adapt things as much as we can. Remember to ask questions and tell us how you feel about things so we can provide the best experience possible. We promise we will let you know which things can't be changed."

Why can't you... stop her labor, save the baby, do a C-section, take care of the baby's body, "put her out" (give her medications), etc.?
"If we could change what is happening, we would. Unfortunately there are some things we can't make better. Other families before you have taught us what is important; we will make sure mother's physical care is our first priority and offer all of you as much comfort as we can."

When do I have to...go to the hospital, get into the bed, change my clothes, decide about the baby, get pain medication, decide about turning off the ventilator, etc.?
"Most things can be done on your time. When you are ready, we'll be here to help you. There are very few things that need to be done at a certain time; for those, we'll let you know as far ahead as possible. Otherwise, it is about when it feels right to you."

CHAPTER FIVE

STRATEGIES: PRACTICING *the* ART *of* CARING

This is a story about a sudden, unexpected death and a family's path in healing.

Gary and Sharon arrived at labor and delivery glowing with that "about to become parents" look. This was the day they waited for all their lives. The typical American couple, they were high school sweethearts and dreamed of their first baby together. They were ready: crib purchased, blankets washed, and dancing princesses on the nursery walls. They calmed as they heard the steady whoosh-whoosh of their baby's heartbeat on the monitor, cherished music to their ears. Family gathered around the bedside and shared stories about their own labors. The grandparents admired modern advances that protected precious babies.

Sharon's labor slowly progressed, so Dr. Lake suggested rupturing the baby's membranes to "move things along." Sharon had read about the procedure in her childbirth books but was still nervous. Both doctor and nurse reassured her and it was done before she knew it. She was one step closer to becoming a mom, she told herself.

Sharon dozed and the room quieted in respect to the laboring mother. Gary listened as the quiet tapping of the heartbeat eerily slowed down. Before he could comprehend what was going on, Sharon and her bed were being pushed through the doorway. The staff spoke in calm voices, but their faces told another story: something was wrong. Gary's requests to go with her were quickly denied. As he helplessly watched his wife's bed speed down the hall, he fell into his mother's arms and waited for news.

The chaplain offered words of reassurance but Gary could not hear them. "My God, what is happening?" he kept repeating. The door finally opened and Dr. Lake stepped in. The family moved closer together as they heard, "The surgery went well and Sharon will be returning to her room soon." He paused, then continued, "I'm sorry, but we lost the baby." Gary sat down hard, stunned. Lost the baby?

Missy, Sharon's nurse, was full of adrenaline. She had been the first to see decelerations on the monitor and knew the baby was in trouble. She mobilized coworkers and got the doctor from the lounge. It took only minutes from the bedside to delivery, but the baby could not be successfully resuscitated. As she prepared to bring Sharon back to the room, she mentally reviewed everything again. Her coworkers were unusually quiet, almost robotic. Everyone was feeling the death of this special baby.

When Missy wheeled Sharon into the room, Gary whispered, "She looks more beautiful than she did this morning, so peaceful. How am I going to tell her?" Missy offered to help, but he wanted to be the one. Others were shepherded out of the room as Sharon roused from post-anesthesia sleep. Gary cradled her pale cheeks in his hands and looked into her eyes. He choked out, "Our beautiful Emily Rose has died." He looked up momentarily at Missy. "Emily Rose. That's the first time I ever said that name out loud. It has been a secret up till now." He looked back at Sharon as she closed her eyes and turned her head. He worried that something was wrong. He had already lost his daughter; he couldn't lose his wife, too. He panicked and asked, "Is she OK?" Missy put her arm around his shoulder and said, "Everyone handles grief in their own way. Maybe Sharon isn't ready yet. It's been a rough few hours."

Outside Sharon's room, family emotions quickly escalated from total surprise to confusion, anger, and tears. Father Bob, the chaplain, tried to move them to a quiet room but they bombarded him with questions and wouldn't budge. "What's going on? How is Sharon? How could you all let this happen?" Gary joined them in the hall. All he could do was accept hugs from those who loved him.

Missy approached Gary and the family about seeing Emily Rose. "We know this has been horrible for you. Would it help to see your daughter? We've prepared a place down the hall so you can spend some time with her," she said. Gary couldn't imagine seeing his daughter cold and lifeless, but when he caught sight of her lying under the soft glow of the warmer, he thought she was the most beautiful thing he had ever seen. First he tenderly touched her cheek, hoping to see life, but when he felt coolness on his fingertips, he knew it was real. He picked her up like a china doll and kissed her. Fr. Bob stayed close by. After a few minutes he gently asked if the grandparents could come in, too.

Throughout the rest of the day, Sharon asked for pain medication and slept. She requested that only Gary and their parents be allowed to visit. Gary spent each minute at her bedside while the grandmothers stood vigil over Emily Rose. Gary was concerned for his wife and fired off questions whenever Missy entered the room. Missy and her coworkers calmly answered each question despite their own nervousness. The feeling in the room was palpable.

Before the end of her shift, Missy asked Gary, "Should we bring the baby for Sharon to see?" They went together to talk with Sharon but got no response, either in words or tears. Staff offered many times during the night, but Sharon continued to retreat to her mental private place. Gary was at a loss about what to do. He was sure that she would fall in love with Emily Rose once she finally saw her. His heart hurt every time he thought about it. Jo, the night nurse, could see that Gary was mentally and physically depleted. She brought him a warm blanket and a glass of juice when he refused to lie down. She tended to Sharon, too, making sure there were no preventable complications. They had been through enough; they didn't need any more pain.

Shifts passed and Sharon did not acknowledge tiny Emily Rose, despite the prodding of family and staff. They would talk about her in front of Sharon and share mementos and pictures. Julie, the bereavement nurse, came to visit each day, but Sharon's reply was the same: "Get that Death Lady out of here." Sharon was recovering physically, but everyone worried about her mentally.

The evening before discharge, Julie decided to try one more time. As she casually talked with family, she noticed Sharon rubbing her stomach, so she asked if she was in pain. "What?" glared Sharon. "I noticed you were rubbing your tummy. Are you in pain?" the nurse asked again. Sharon began asking each person in the room "Did you see me rubbing my tummy? DID YOU SEE ME RUBBING MY TUMMY?" Each request was louder and more demanding until she said to the nurse, "DON'T YOU KNOW I STILL THINK SHE IS IN THERE!" Sharon began to sob as the room went silent. "Bring her to me," was all she could get

out. Gary carried Emily Rose to her mother. Sharon
reached for her as they walked through the door.

The next hours were spent reveling in Emily Rose, holding
and rocking her. Julie took lots of photos and a blessing
ceremony was done. They bathed her again and changed
her clothes. Emily spent the night in a bassinette between
her parents so she could be touched and loved. She was
their perfect Emily Rose.

The next morning, Julie was welcomed into the room, not
shooed away as before. Together, they spoke of Sharon's
need to be suspended in time. They talked of hopes and
dreams, too, of Emily Rose and her dancing princess walls.
When they were ready, Julie gently helped them say
goodbye. Each kissed her and Gary handed her to Julie. She
promised to continue to take good care of sweet Emily Rose.
Gary and Sharon dreaded leaving the safe shelter of the
hospital and going home to an empty crib. Julie escorted
them to their car, carefully avoiding the usual exit used
by other new families. Sharon asked, "When we have a
service, will you come? You were a part of Emily Rose, too."
Julie considered it a privilege to be asked.

Julie ran into Dr. Lane the next day. "What was it, three
days? How did you get her to see that baby?" he asked.
Julie thought for a moment "I think it was in the timing.
She had a lot of grieving to do before she could see her
daughter. I'm just glad it happened before she left." Dr.
Lane was quiet as he considered that. "Maybe you're right,
but it was about being consistent—you visiting everyday,
helping her get there."

Emily Rose was buried on a beautiful September day. Gary carried the tiny casket to the graveside. The family gathered close and sang "Amazing Grace." In such a few days, each one had said hello and goodbye. That moment was filled with love.

It is a lofty vision that leads us to the bedside. There is something about the intimacy of caring for the body that translates to caring about the soul as well. The piece of our personality that brought us to our profession is the same one that encourages us to "fix it and make it all better." How can we help families walk away with anything positive when their baby dies? It is an awesome responsibility when our care impacts the quality of parents' healing.

There is a fine line between caretakers and caregivers: care*takers* feel responsible for the outcome, while care*givers* allow the path to take its own direction. If we choose to companion families experiencing a perinatal loss, we will become true caregivers and guides for the journey. As with any good guide, we must be well prepared, ready for opportunities and challenges as they arise.

Setting goals for the journey

Grief care starts at admission, diagnosis, delivery, and/or death. What are the most important elements of care? What will make a difference hours, weeks or months from now? If we had a crystal ball, we could list each item; unfortunately, there is no magical method.

Medical personnel have been trained to think assessment, planning, intervention and evaluation. If the family is to lead the way, how can we follow that process? Our care plan must make the traditional regulations and procedures more like keys, hanging on a heavy ring, ready for any door that needs opening. One simple objective prepares and fuels us for the tough and intense journey ahead:

To offer the family the most positive experience possible after the death of their baby or loss of their pregnancy.

The family is the only one that can define what is "positive." As we draw closer and walk alongside, we begin to see what is important to them. After Sharon and Gary lost their baby, it was hard to sort out what could be positive in all the anger, shock and confusion. As hours and days passed, Gary, Sharon and their parents taught their caregivers that healing began when they were ready—and not a minute sooner. For them, the most positive piece of the experience was having the time and flexibility they needed. Can you imagine the ending to the story if the staff stuck to their usual routines?

Bringing direction to the bedside role

Companioning expands our role in making the family's experience the very best it can be. Our bedside practice will still involve traditional standards such as:

- Providing physical care to the mother and support to her family.
- Assuring the labor process flows as smoothly as possible, avoiding complications.
- Offering options for saying goodbye.

Companioning expands those tasks as it urges us to go deeper. We reformat our thinking to include:

- Offering a safe and respectful environment in which the family can explore and express their grief as they choose.
- Gently leading family in overcoming their fears so they can make choices and decisions that will be healing for them.
- Being available and present for family so care can happen when they are ready.
- Offering time for family to tell their story in words and in behaviors.
- Communicating with other members of the healthcare team about the family's wishes.

- Role modeling mourning behaviors and helping family understand it is OK to grieve.
- Providing moments where the life of their baby is celebrated as well as mourned.
- Offering tangible mementos as a way of honoring their baby while bridging the gap between hospital and home.

Many caregivers already provide these concepts in their care. The difference, when thinking about companioning, is that these tenets *become* the care. They are first on the list.

Companioning in motion

Coming to the hospital can be the darkest part of the family's grieving journey. It may have started in the doctor's office, ultrasound suite or triage cart; their next steps happen in an unknown place, with strangers as their only guides.

Their pain surrounds and infiltrates every facet of bedside care. We wish we didn't have to witness their pain. If we could, we would cut it away or suppress its symptoms. Pain is part of the journey and companioning teaches us to be present to the grieving person and their pain. "Being present" sounds simple. When we are at the bedside, aren't we present? Isn't just physically being there enough? More than being in the same space, being present changes us from spectators to participants. We become part of the story while still maintaining our own character. Our attitude is one of "I am here for you." Being present means giving yourself completely for a moment in time.

Presence grows from our instinctive caring. It comes when we shed our professional coats and enter into the family's experience. At first, you may have to work at being present. After a while, it will flow naturally. When first practicing presence, keep these things in mind:

- *Initiate the kind of relationship that will get them through their experience.* They need a liaison, a guide. Your words and behaviors should say, "I want to be here, I want to help." An aura of trust helps them to feel safe in an unfamiliar place.

- *Be flexible, especially in the initial hours.* Stay close and adapt schedules and procedures when needed. Make the plan be about them, not the hospital.

- *Honor their need to be "suspended"* as they are caught in the numbness of grief. It is OK to become suspended with them, allowing periods of inactivity and quiet. Sometimes the gift of stillness is the best you can offer.

- *Physical touch connects and energizes.* Your arm around their shoulder may be the strength they need.

- *Be the consistent and unassuming force in the room.* Their compass may be swirling in circles, but your compass points to calm.

- *Listen to their story, in words and actions.* It will tell you what being present means to them.

Being present to the family and believing in their ability to survive is the foundation to all bedside strategies. The care that evolves from being present is what makes the difference.

Admission: the first steps of the journey

In the first hours, parents are in the midst of new, raw grief and don't hear very well, see very well, or feel very well. They need something to figuratively (and sometimes literally) hold them up. They need to be the total focus of someone who will go the extra mile. How can we make those initial steps as positive as possible?

Make a contact before they come to the hospital (when it is known that death is going to happen at or soon after birth.) A call before admission offers the family time to think about options and sets the beginning of the relationship. Ask them to share their story if they can and offer answers to questions they might be reluctant to ask. Let them know the staff is willing to be with them during this overwhelming time. Emma, a mother whose unborn baby died at 16 weeks, felt her pre-call made all the difference. "I knew what to expect. The nurse also told me about the miscarriage burial. I worried about that, but didn't know how to ask." Emma came to the hospital knowing her baby was going to be treated with respect, something that was healing for her. A pre-admission call can be done by any member of the team and is best done by one who will meet the family on admission.

Make the room a place of respite and security. If the patient is diagnosed in a triage or holding area, transfer her to a private room as soon as possible. Consider bypassing the recovery room and returning to the patient room after surgery. Find a separate, calming place for extended family to wait other than the conventional waiting area. Make their place one that says "you are safe here."

Assess the immediate needs of the patient and the family. What do they understand? What do they need right now? The death of Gary and Sharon's baby came unexpectedly. Staff could not bombard them with information or make assumptions about how they were feeling; rather, they had to work towards understanding where they were at that moment and what they needed.

Respect the confusion and disorder. When families are first admitted, time seems chaotic and choppy. Usually logical admission procedures and post-op routines go haywire and the patient room fills with disorder—physically, mentally and spiritually. Tolerate the confusion and look for moments of clarity to interject assessment questions and bits of information. Even though her family embraced the death of Emily Rose, Sharon needed to live within her own private world. Eventually, her mind was able to clear the path and come to terms with what had happened. Staff had to work on Sharon's time, not theirs. Gary, on the other hand, lived in a separate chaos. Supporting Sharon and Gary was certainly a challenge for the staff.

Focus on the physical issues first. Families need to feel comfortable in their surroundings before moving on to more personal issues.

Concrete issues are easier to approach before abstract ones. Limit information at first, answering questions as they arise. If the mother is in labor or labor is to be induced, physical care must be the priority. Trust-filled relationships built while offering physical care will aid in conversations about more sensitive issues later.

Be prepared. There is nothing more frustrating than to walk into a situation and stumble with words or tasks. Before entering a room, run through a mental checklist. How will you begin the conversation? What supplies will you need? What alterations to the environment need to be done? If you are nervous or distracted, it will add to the family's confusion.

Companioning: the next hours

Bereavement care may last for hours and days in obstetrics. As the family begins to grasp what has happened and open up to their grief, the level of bedside care changes. Families are unable to attend to themselves, let alone their baby. Our continuing care helps them in the long haul of the next few days. Every family creates a unique and personal memory; our part becomes setting the opportunity and supplying the tools. Remember to:

Involve the whole team. Bereavement care can be offered by many caregivers, each bringing a unique perspective and connection to the family. If we offer care from many different angles, the family can gravitate to the one that feels best to them. Caregivers may be of different disciplines or many people of the same discipline. It took a whole village to care for Gary and Sharon in the three days after the death of Emily Rose—doctors, chaplains, labor nurses, postpartum nurses, bereavement support nurses and unit support staff. Each had a special part.

Guide them in saying hello before they consider saying goodbye. Help the family complete the crossover from prenatal relationship to postnatal relationship. Families need guidance in seeing and being with their baby; they need help in separating the pain of loss from the actual baby, at least for a short time. Set an atmosphere that makes the baby the first priority and death secondary. Create deliberate moments of bonding such as holding, bathing, dressing, etc, and invite all to participate as they are comfortable. It may help to physically show them the way. Rita, a seasoned labor nurse, creates a ritual of the baby's bath. She sets a quiet and soothing setting in the middle of the room, lays out extra wash cloths on the edge of the bassinette. As she talks and coos to the baby, she tenderly tests the water for temperature. She begins the bath slowly and deliberately and invites family to draw closer. Eventually, she involves family members in bathing and dressing. Many families will be afraid; they will only see a dead body rather than their beloved baby. They need someone to help them over-come their fears so they can love their baby at this special time.

Treat the baby as you would any other, with respect and dignity. Something as simple as carrying their baby in your arms rather than a bassinette or basket shows the family that their baby is worth the gift of touch. Always refer to the baby by name (if the family has chosen one), even before birth. Appropriately sized clothing and blankets transmit the message that their baby is "a real baby," not a "miscarriage" or "fetus." Emily Rose was dressed each time her family saw her. She was like any other baby, right down to her ID bracelet. Emily Rose deserved to be treated like a baby.

Let the family set the timing. They will let you know, by words and behaviors, when they are ready to take in more information or tackle the overwhelming tasks of saying hello and goodbye. Gently introduce subjects as needed and answer questions. Concentrate on offering small bits of information and assure they understand what is happening in a style and pace that is acceptable to them. Some families may need encouragement to slow down and fight the instinct to speed up the process and make impulsive decisions. Use your intuition to help set the pace and keep options open for further experiences. When JaQuan died a few hours after delivery, Leesa and Bobby spent about two hours with him. Bobby told the nurse they "were done" and were ready for him to go to the morgue. The next day, Leesa asked to see JaQuan again, but he had already been sent to another facility for autopsy. Any opportu-nities for the family to spend time with JaQuan were gone. He had

CHOOSING CLOTHING FOR BABY

- Baby should be dressed in a gown or sleeper, blanket, and bonnet or hat. Avoid burial gowns; baby should look like a baby when dressed.
- All clothing should be appropriately sized; nothing makes a baby look more small and insignificant than an outfit or blanket that is too big.
- Clothing should have easy access for parents to see all of baby as they are ready.
- Colors should be soft and muted, easy on the eye. Parents love their baby girls in pink and their boys in blue. Try to avoid dark colors for babies with dark coloring. Some cultures prefer brighter colors or all white. When possible, let the family select the clothes for their baby.
- Clothing can add texture to the parent's sensory experience. Soft flannel and fleece feel good to the fingertips. Knitted or crocheted blankets add dimension.
- Baby should wear a diaper, ready-made or from a sterile gauze square.

died so quickly, the family was not able to think clearly. Because of this family's experience, the hospital implemented a policy that babies do not leave the facility until the mother is discharged.

Facilitate support systems that provide comfort. Ask the parents, "Who can help you during this tough time?" Offer to make calls or adapt visiting policies so family and friends can provide the kind of support that will continue after they leave the hospital. Latoya, a teen mom who delivered a 22-week gestation baby, had more than 50 visitors during her 16-hour stay. After listening to her story, the chaplain understood that Latoya's pregnancy was a rite of passage in her social group because all of her friends had babies. She suggested that Latoya invite her friends to "meet" her baby. Latoya let each one hold her tiny baby and showed off his little footprint molds and Polaroid pictures. Latoya needed her support system—her teen friends—to be a part of her experience. She needed to be assured that she would still be a part of the social group, despite her loss. The chaplain also called Latoya's pastor, who came and blessed the baby. Although Latoya did not know her pastor well, she appreciated his time with her baby. That began a new relationship of support for her.

Continue to provide physical care while meeting the bereavement needs of each family member. Remember to offer the kind of care that any postpartum mother would receive, balancing physical components with emotional ones. Even if the mother was just 15 weeks pregnant, she had a delivery and is at risk for complications such as hemorrhage and infection. A patient may deliver at 24 weeks but still have engorgement. All patients deserve the same standard of care. Care should be taken in choosing the location for postpartum care. Many facilities automatically transfer newly delivered mothers to non-OB units, thinking that the sights and sounds of OB increase grief. However, the opposite can be true. Ginger was transferred to a medical unit after she delivered a 21-week gestation baby. Her doctor told her "it would be too painful to hear the babies cry." She told the bereavement nurse the next day, "It's funny, I heard the babies crying all through labor and nobody ever worried about that. Actually, I thought it was kind of comforting to know that somebody in the next room was happy."

Ginger also said, "These (medical unit) nurses are really nice, but I don't think they get it. They don't ask about the baby and they give me a pain pill when I cry." Families should be given options, whenever possible, about the location of their postpartum care, after laying out pros and cons of staying in OB (with caregivers who understand vs. the reminders of delivery). When given the choice, most families choose to stay in OB.

Consider the whole family as "the patient." While family members (besides the mother) do not have the physical experience of delivery, they may still carry the physical/emotional side effects of grief and may need care for grief-related symptoms. Sharon's postpartum nurse understood that Gary was a part of Sharon's care; she encouraged him to rest and hydrate along with offering him her words of comfort. Extended family members and friends often need suggestions in how to be helpful during this time, whether it is at the bedside or caring for matters at home. All need our compassion and direction.

Remember the power of kindness. The simplest things can make a difference: answering the call light quickly, offering "real" tissues instead of the standard hospital variety, making sure there is access to coffee, offering pain medication before they ask. These are the things that will remain in a parent's memory. Tricia, a mother whose baby died in NICU, offered this memory: "One day towards the end, I fell asleep with my head leaning on his incubator. When I woke up, I had a blanket around my shoulders. I can't tell you how warm and comforting that was."

Letting them lead the way

It's hard for caregivers to work off the cuff. We want something to tell us when and what to do. Care strategies in bereavement care can't always be boxed in and checked off. Most will flow from our general willingness to be part of the experience. We carry opportunities in our hearts rather than on our flow charts.

Sometimes, though, no matter how hard we try, families resist our strategies for care. Tom and Sarah knew their baby would die soon after birth. They contacted a support nurse prior to admission and had read about delivering a baby who would die. They came to the hospital with the decision not to see, hold or name their baby. Many staff members tried to gently coax them into reconsidering, but they would not budge. During a follow-up call, Sarah told the nurse, "It isn't that I regret not seeing him, but I wish you would have tried harder." Sarah needed support over the next few months to help her realize that she and Tom made the best decision at the time. The staff offered opportunities for Sarah and Tom to embrace the birth and death of their baby. It was their choice to decline.

We will never know if our bedside care made a difference for most families. Because of their inability to express themselves, many will not be able to tell us in words or actions if we have been helpful. Penny's sixth child was stillborn. During the postpartum period she was quiet and distant, holding the baby a few times but mostly sleeping. She declined the offer for family pictures and put her baby's mementos in her suitcase. Staff felt they had failed in their care because they hadn't "gotten through." Three months later, Penny sent back a note with a hospital survey that said, "I could not believe how kind everyone was. I couldn't have made it without them. I would recommend your hospital to anyone. I was blessed to have those people with me at such a tough time." Sometimes strategies are a matter of faith. If we enter into the family's journey and let them lead the way, it will make a difference.

OPTIONS FOR CARE

- Seeing and holding their baby
- Spending unlimited time with their baby, as it feels right to them. It may be continuous until discharge or the baby can come and go as they need.
- Parenting their baby—bathing, dressing, etc
- Naming their baby. This includes paternity paperwork.
- Having any ceremonies or rituals that fit within their religion or culture
- Collecting mementos to remember their baby
- Having supportive people available, whether it be family, friends or personnel from the hospital
- Receiving information about post-mortem studies and time to make decisions
- Receiving information about grief and loss in both written and verbal form
- Choosing location of hospital room post-loss

CHAPTER SIX

MEMORIES: MAKING *the* MOMENT LAST *a* LIFETIME

This is a story about a precious baby who will always live in the hearts of his parents.

Nita and Don struggled throughout their first pregnancy. Nita had been sent to bed in her 4th month for premature rupture of the membranes. Each day she remained pregnant added to their dream. If she could just get to 28 weeks, they both said, everything would be all right. Nita delivered at 29.2 weeks. Although Jacob had breathing problems at first, they were filled with hope. (Days of bed rest will do that, according to Nita.) But little Jacob's lungs weren't developed enough and he died of respiratory failure when he was four hours old. Days and months of waiting and hoping were dashed in minutes.

Nita and Don loved children! Nita was a preschool teacher at the local church. Children were both her career and her passion. Her students had taught her the power of love between parent and child. Now she felt hollow—empty without that love she had patiently waited for. She and Don talked about Jacob a lot. Even though their precious baby was not physically with them, they both felt his spirit. They would never have finger paintings on the refrigerator or Wal-Mart photos on the mantel, but they did have mementos that the nurses had lovingly made for them before he died. They had laid them out on the dining table the day Nita was discharged from the hospital and liked to look at and touch them. Don would often burrow his face in Jacob's tiny blanket so he "would never forget the smell of his son." Cards and flowers were scattered among the molds and footprints.

As the weeks passed and the numbness wore away, the disorder of the house started to bother them. As they stacked newspapers and sorted mail, they talked about what to do with Jacob's things. The chaplain at the hospital had assured them it was OK to keep Jacob's memories visible as long as they wanted, but they wondered if he "deserved more" than a life scattered among wilting flowers and sympathy cards. Before they knew it, they had put pencil to paper, designing a cabinet for Jacob. With the help of Don's dad, they made Jacob's cabinet with their own hands.

Jacob's cabinet sat in the living room next to the TV. Five feet tall with lighted shelves and glassed sides, it was a tribute to love. All "his little things"—gown and hat, molds of hands and feet, name bracelet, blessing card and angel pin—were carefully housed there. Two of their favorite pictures were in sterling silver frames, one right after he was born and one after he died, when he was "dressed in his finest." A set of alphabet blocks spelled out his whole name, Jacob Ernest Murphy. ("You can't imagine how many packages we had to buy to get the letters in colors we wanted," Nita said later.) They even framed a piece of fetal monitoring strip, scripted while "he was still inside and safe." It took them weeks to create this tribute of love. They put the cabinet in the living room where they spent most of their waking hours and gathered when company came. They wanted everyone who came through the door to see "Jacob's place."

When Nita and Don talked about the cabinet after the hospital's candle lighting service, another mother asked, "What do other people say when they see it? I've been

afraid to put Jeffrey's things out for fear that no one would
notice or would shy away." Nita told her, "There are people
who come in and say nothing. The cabinet is big enough it
can't be missed—like the elephant in the room. But some
ask and want to know about Jacob. They are amazed at
the hand molds and want to touch them. I take them out
and show them off. I absolutely love it! I am so proud of
my little boy, I want everyone to know!" Another mother
overheard Nita and joined in: "You're lucky. I got only a
blanket and a blessing card." Nita told her, "Be creative
and let your heart lead the way. It isn't about the stuff; it's
about the love that inspires it."

It has been four years since Jacob was born, and "his place"
still sits in honor next to the TV. The Murphys had
another child 18 months after Jacob died. Her name is
Jessica and she lights their life. Nita is now expecting
again—this time another boy. Both Nita and Don proudly
announce this will be their third child. Jacob was too
important to be left out.

Memories are triggers, linking to what has already come, allowing
the past to become real again for a short while. Our refrigerators,
bulletin boards and dressers become sacred spaces that keep us
connected to a time that felt good. Many families in perinatal loss
come upon situations that have no place among those altars of
mementos. Many have never experienced death up-close-and-per-
sonal. They have no skills in how to glean the bad from the good,
the life-embracing from the life-troubling. Regardless, they still
make memories, whether they feel safe or not.

As caregivers, we are given the awesome responsibility of witness-
ing the memories a family makes of their tiny baby. We hold the
light in the wilderness. Our beam says, "Look here and remember

something besides the pain." We don't create the memories; we simply help imprint them.

Sensual memories

A memory is anything that brings an indescribable feeling to the surface. They come in all shapes and sizes, some that can be touched, some a recollection. A memory may be purposefully pulled from the past or float into the present with a familiar sense in the air. It may bring with it a smile to the face, a stirring in the chest, or tears to the eyes.

Memories are recorded by the senses of sight, hearing, touch, smell, and taste. When a baby dies, responses of parents go askew. The five senses go into overtime, working hard to record what they are seeing and feeling. They will remember the blueness of the room, the fuzziness of the blanket, the gentleness of a caregiver's voice. Those memories last forever.

Our care can enhance the senses to aid family in absorbing positive memories. Don told of wanting to smell his son's blanket. For him, each breath stimulated additional visual and tactile memories, such as how Jacob felt in his arms, the shape of his perfect nose, and the smoothness of his fingernails. Because caregivers encouraged those sensual experiences, Don and Nita took home more than a baby blanket. They took precious moments, too.

Some memories are tangible. You can physically see, hold, smell, or hear them. They are monuments to moments we don't want to forget. Nita and Don needed to see and touch Jacob's bonnet and booties, hand molds and ID bracelet to stay connected to him. They used Jacob's mementos as a way to open the story: see how precious my Jacob was. Tangible mementos make a baby even more special.

Most memories have no form. Intangible memories—those without physical boundaries—are shaped and interpreted by the person choosing to remember. Jeremy, a father of a premature baby who died in the NICU, had never held a baby before he held his two-pound son. "I expected him to feel as light as a feather, but his lit-

INTANGIBLE MEMORIES

Examples of remembrances from parents

- Holding her for the first time
- Watching my family hold her, too
- Giving him a bath; watching my mother give him a bath
- How she felt wrapped in the blanket my grandmother made
- The baby shampoo—smell of her silky hair
- His big-boy hands wrapped around his little teddy bear
- The baptismal water as the priest poured it over her head
- The sound of his name spoken by others

tle body pressed against my chest. Sometimes when I can't sleep, I can feel it again." Parent's stories often include moments such as seeing their baby tucked in Grandpa's arms, having a blessing cere- mony, or receiving an unexpected visit from a friend. Grieving families may not be aware of intangible memories, but they are the glue that connects tiny bits of their experience together. Intangible memories coupled with tangible memories make a lifetime of dif- ference. It is our job as caregivers to create opportunities for both.

Involving the whole family in making memories

During the acute time of loss, there is a profound need to bring families and friends together. Each needs a special kind of comfort and solace. Each needs to feel safe in making their own personal memories. Each contributes to the pool of memories in which the baby is the tiny pebble that creates ripples of love. From the doting grandmother to the helpful neighbor to the cashier who comment- ed weekly about mother's growing belly, all will be changed by the experience.

Family and friends often don't know how to participate in the baby's life and support the parents; they so badly want to help but are unsure what to do. Caregivers can direct extended family and friends and invite them to participate with the parents' OK. All family members can participate in loving baby. Cheryl's friend Allison precipitously delivered her baby at 21 weeks. Cheryl came immediately when Allison called and was shocked to see the baby in the room. Watching her friend cradle her tiny daughter, Cheryl began to understand the importance of having the baby close by. When Allison asked her if she would like to hold the baby, she accepted. The nurse took a picture of the three of them together and Allison gave her a copy to keep. Having her best friend a part of her baby's life was a priceless memory for Allison.

Enhancing moments

The first impression is often the most lasting. For grieving parents, the strongest memory may be the first time they saw their baby.

Although we may have hours and days to shape and mold memories, there will be only one *first time* for them to meet their tiny baby. When possible, it is important that the moment be chosen by the parents. It may be immediately after delivery or death, or it may be days later. The parents choose when it is right for them. It is our privilege to enhance the moment.

- *At delivery, wrap baby in a warm blanket.* Non-traditional hospital blankets and stocking caps create a softer look. Brenda and Justin's baby died minutes after birth due to a rare birth defect. The circulating nurse wrapped her in a pink blanket and cap. Brenda remembered the pink standing out from the hospital surgical green, a comforting memory. If possible, dim overhead lights and play quiet music in the background. Trina's baby, David Lee, was born still after an hour of pushing. The soap operas were playing on the TV and although she wasn't watching them, the sound imprinted. Trina was anxious for months whenever they were on and had no idea why. Jessica's baby was born as a lullaby CD was playing. "I loved that James came into this world with his own music," she said. She bought a copy of the CD and played it at his funeral because it was "his music."

- *The warmth and soft light of the warmer can create an inviting place for baby* if the family is not ready to see baby immediately. Family can come to baby when they are ready.

- *After the bath, dress the baby in baby colors and subtle textures.* The first time parents see their baby dressed, it is important the baby *look* like a baby rather than a dead body. When Gary, the father of Emily Rose, saw her lying under the soft glow of the warmer, he thought she was the most beautiful thing he had ever seen. She was not laid out like a body at a funeral home; she was dressed and positioned like a sleeping baby.

- *Keep baby as free from dampness as possible.* If baby's skin is seeping, line the inside of the gown with a disposable diaper or absorbent gauze and change it often. Parents want to remember their baby as warm and dry, like all babies.

Creating ceremony as memories

A ceremony is a time dedicated to the celebration of something or
someone special. Our families of origin impart the importance and
meaning of ceremony: it is how we become an official part of the
world. When a baby dies, however, dreams of ceremonies fade.
There will be no bridal dress flowing down the aisle, no diploma
hanging on the wall. Even special baby ceremonies are missing: no
christening or baptism, no choosing of godparents. Families
mourn over these rites of passage along with the loss of their baby.

What we must remember, however, is that ceremonies can still be
created within the hospital walls. Ceremonies evolve when the pri-
mary attitude is "here is someone special who deserves our attention." In cases of perinatal loss, in-hospital ceremonies can be formal, such as baptism, or informal, such as a family photo. During
family moments, focus on creating ceremony. Gather family around
the baby, soften the light, and exaggerate the movement. Something
as simple as bringing the baby into the room in a basket lined with
a lacy blanket, laying down the basket in the middle of the bed, and
gently handing him to his parents can be seen as ceremony if it is
done with a "I am presenting this baby to you" flourish. Tangible
items connect and enhance the memory. For example, a small shell
can hold the droplets of holy water for a baptism and can then
become a keepsake for parents.

Parents often push themselves to focus on post-death ceremonies
while still in the hospital. Family members encourage them to
hurry the process to provide "closure" or "get it over with."
Parents need to take their time and find healing in funerals and
memorial services because it is one thing they can begin to control
in a world that feels totally out of control. They need to plan a
service that tells the story of their baby, no matter how brief the
story seems.

Caregivers can offer two precious gifts: suggestions about how to
create a personalized service for baby and the time the family
needs to make decisions. Parents can begin to create ceremony
within the safe environment of the hospital and continue it, when
they are ready, at home. Rhonda and Jim could not bring them-

selves to go home without some kind of ceremony. Their church did not believe in infant baptism and the blessing didn't seem like enough. The grief support nurse helped them arrange a "memorial time" in the hospital's chapel before they went home. Family and friends gathered to have a prayer service in baby's honor. Their baby was cremated two days later, and in the spring they had a tree planting ceremony "just for Jamie." Some families may gravitate to a formal service, some a graveside service, some a poem reading or prayer in their back yard. Ceremony is a part of healing and uniquely theirs.

Taking photos

Parents are often unsure about photographs. Most want to decline. To them, a photo would only capture the intense pain they are feeling and serve as a reminder that will never go away. It seems unnatural to take pictures of a dead person because in most North American cultures, that is not done when other loved ones die.

Julie and Jon delivered a 27-week gestation stillborn; both felt pictures were "unnecessary and morbid" and instructed the nurse not to take any. Seven years later, Julie called the hospital to inquire about mementos. After researching the case, the support nurse told her there was nothing. Julie's nurse had carefully documented the offer for photos three times and the patient's response. Julie, ready to think about her baby born long ago, cried, "Why did she believe me?"

Cindy was a mother of a baby with multiple visible birth defects. Her baby was so disfigured that the nurse decided photos weren't possible. When Cindy came to support group and saw other parents' photos, she asked if there were pictures of her baby. The leader told her there were none. Cindy responded, "Do you mean to tell me that my baby was such a monster that no one would take a picture of her?"

Parents like Julie and Cindy have taught staff the lesson of setting a standard of care: photos are to be taken of all babies who die. Photos help families to continue their journey through the dark wilderness. A photo helps jog a family's memory as they see their baby's first bath or baptism frozen in time. Photos provide a sensual trigger, too: dad's tender touch of his baby's cheek; the silkiness of her hair; the longing in mother's eyes as she cuddles with baby. Most of all, a photo can give families something to share with others. "See his tiny feet and sweet face? My baby was a baby, too." A photograph creates a sense of who their baby was and makes their baby real.

For most caregivers, the task of taking photos of dead or dying babies carries much responsibility and anxiety: there is only one opportunity to get it right. With a little work and creativity, we can take the kind of pictures that capture a lifetime on film:

- *Stage a place to take pictures.* Remove hospital equipment and create a backdrop by draping a baby blanket over the warmer. Make the background one of softness and safety.

- *Consider lighting:* Standard hospital room light will give a clear, distinct photo, while a warmer/exam light will give a soft tone. Natural light lightens baby. The best photos offer pictures in a variety of lights.

- *Choose clothing that complements the baby's coloring,* such as medium pinks or blues. Avoid very light colors and busy/big prints. Use a variety of textures to give contrast.

- *Position the baby in natural poses,* just as you would other newborns: lying on her side with hands near her face; on his tummy, his little feet tucked under his bottom where they belong. Avoid gaping mouths and the "laid out in a casket look." Take at least one picture of baby unclothed, for family will want to remember every inch of their baby. Do full body shots and close-ups of baby's face, hands and feet. Babies should look comfortable and loved.

- *Offer family photos.* Many families will decline when asked, thinking those moments are too painful, and then regret their decision later. Have a camera ready and take spontaneous photos when possible. Parents cherish photos of their babies snuggled safely in their arms.

• *Size-appropriate props can accent the baby* and give depth and interest to the picture: small stuffed animals; blocks that spell out baby's name; silk roses; the baby's footprint card or ring. An angel figure or fuzzy teddy bear watching over baby adds comfort. Take care that props don't overwhelm the photo and become the focus, however. One hospital discarded most of their props when a parent told them their baby "looked like he was on a garage sale table." Props are meant to accent the baby, not the other way around. Some items used in the pictures can be placed in the baby's Memory Keeper to continue the sensual connection later.

• *Some babies don't appear to be very photographable* because of extreme small size, maceration or birth defects. Light amounts of powder or blush to fragile skin, special positioning and softer lighting can lessen the look. Even if the baby wasn't perfect, parents see through the eyes of unconditional love and will often focus on features we do not see.

• *If using 35mm film with delayed processing,* also take pictures with a Polaroid or digital camera so family can have pictures to take home right away. They will be a lifeline during the first few days at home.

Collecting other mementos to keep

Owning material things is a measure of value in our society. Perinatal loss parents already struggle with the worth of their baby. He was so small or she never got to come home; will others see how important he was or understand how much we loved her? Nita and Don wanted everyone to see Jacob as they did, as someone worth knowing and loving. Fortunately they had tangible items to display in their cabinet. When others touched the 3-D molds, they would say out loud, "Look at the fingernails and lines in his hand!" What they were thinking was, "He had hands like other babies." The mold helped to make Jacob a real person.

PHOTOGRAPHIC EQUIPMENT: WHAT'S RIGHT FOR YOUR UNIT?

- **Polaroid**: A quick way to give pictures. Can also be a great tool for introducing their baby, if family is reluctant. Easy to use; cost per picture is about $1.00.
- **Disposable**: Convenient, usually sold in the hospital gift shop or nearby drug store. Choose only name brands; off brands have recycled batteries that can cause photos to be dark.
- **35 mm**: A flexible way to take photos; depending on system, can be creative with lighting, speed, and distance. Used in the many lighting systems—fluorescent, indirect, warmer light, etc. Film must be developed outside of hospital. Families will receive negatives for copies.
- **Digital**: Has endless possibilities, especially if a photo printer is readily available. Most have capability of printing pictures in black and white. Cost for buying system and supplies high, especially if institution has a high breakage or theft rate. Families will not receive negatives to make additional copies, but pictures can be placed on a CD or e-mailed.
- **Standard newborn photo service**: Many companies are sympathetic to grieving families and will provide a photo package at no cost. Their service is always available and can be done by trained professionals. They usually pick the package and do not offer any negatives. Additional pictures may be costly.

Each facility will have its own standard of mementos. There is no correct list. Mementos can be anything that touched their baby or could trigger the sensual moments they wish to remember. Parents tell us they especially appreciate:

- **Those that give perspective**, such as the baby's measuring tape, ink foot and handprints, the right-sized blanket. Parents absolutely love 2-D and 3-D molds because they provide wonderful definition of the hands and feet. Although they are "a bit more work," as one nurse terms them, "they are worth every minute they take." There are a variety of mediums and/or kits available from both craft stores and hospital vendors to create molds.

- **Those that physically touched their baby**, such as a lock of hair, the diaper she wore, his own blanket and clothes. Some caregivers want to wash clothes before giving them to family if there has been seepage, but parents should always be consulted first. One father said, "The stuff on his sleeper is the marker he left behind."

- **Those with his or her name**, such as a crib card, name bead bracelet, baby blocks, etc. Documents with baby's whole name such as a blessing card or complimentary birth certificate make the name look "official." Depending on the kinds of support they have once they go home, parents may not hear their baby's name very often. Seeing the name in print can be very comforting.

Creating a holder for memories

Having a sacred space to house the mementos is very important to families. Loose pieces hastily placed in a plastic sack somehow lessen their importance and implies that baby lived a transient life. When mementos are placed in a special holder or keeper, it creates a vessel for memories as they are transferred from hospital to home.

Memory Keepers come in all shapes, sizes and materials. They can be purchased from bereavement care vendors or handmade by volunteers or staff. They can be as ornate as a hand-painted box or as simple as a flannel envelope with a ribbon tie. It doesn't really mat-

MEMENTOS THAT SHOULD BE INCLUDED IN EVERY BABY'S MEMORY KEEPER:

- Appropriately sized clothing—gown, bonnet, blanket, and diaper
- Ink footprints and/or handprints
- Measuring tape
- Crib card, with height and weight documented
- Lock of hair (with family permission)
- ID bracelet
- Photos—instant/digital/35 mm

Ideas for other mementos to add:
- Hand and/or foot molds—2-D and 3-D
- Baby ring
- Angel pin
- Naming bracelet/ name blocks
- Baptismal certificate and shell
- Blessing card
- Bottle of baby shampoo/ soap
- Complimentary birth certificate
- Inspirational sayings or poems
- Videos of baby
- Copies of music played at the bedside

ter what they look like, only that they have the capacity to safely hold the memories. Many families, like Nita and Don, will create their own sacred space for memories when they get home. Some will choose to store their memories in the holder given to them at the hospital. Our gift is not the quality of the Keeper; it is our willingness to honor and value their baby and their memories.

Becoming the keeper of mementos

Some families are not ready to take their mementos when they go home. Perhaps the pain is too overwhelming or physical mementos do not touch their hearts. Parents should be assured that their baby's mementos will be tucked away in a safe place and never discarded. Hospitals should create a space for keeping mementos in the event that family might request them later. Emily and Adam refused all mementos and photos after she delivered an 18-week gestation baby with Down syndrome. They had decided to terminate the pregnancy after learning the diagnosis. Many family members and friends questioned their decision but they were adamant. They came to the hospital wanting to "get it over with" and chose not to hold him or name him. Three years later, Emily called the support nurse to ask about "the baby's things." During the conversation, the nurse asked Emily what had brought her to call today. Emily told the nurse she had had another baby just a few weeks ago, a healthy little girl. "I guess having her safe in my arms made me think about him. Until now, I tried not to think of him as my baby, too. I want Adrianne to know she had a brother." Some families may never ask for their mementos, but it is our role as their companion to offer our ability to help when they are ready.

Memories are everlasting

Caregivers collect memories, too. As the holder of the light in the wilderness, we also absorb memories during the experience. Each one of us could tell the story of a family or baby that deeply touched us. Although we quietly and quickly move on to the next patient, those moments imprint with us. We will never forget their baby or the family.

CHAPTER SEVEN

DISCHARGE: PREPARING *for the* WORK *of* MOURNING

This is a story about a mom who wasn't sure about traveling the next path of the journey.

Brittany had done her best to take care of herself, but she worked full-time and was a single parent of two children. Duane, boyfriend and father of her children, was stationed overseas. At her 34-week checkup, Brittany's blood pressure was 198/115. Her doctor told her to go to labor and delivery immediately for medication and possible early delivery. She made calls as she left the office, picked her kids up from school and got them settled with friends. Her children had to be taken care of first.

Brittany arrived at labor and delivery three hours later with sky-high blood pressure and a massive headache. The nurses couldn't find the baby's heartbeat. An ultrasound confirmed the baby had died sometime between the doctor's office and hospital. Diagnosed with pre-eclampsia, Brittany had IV magnesium sulfate started immediately. Her life turned upside down as she struggled with a crushing headache and broken heart. She was C-sectioned six hours after admission when her blood pressure could not be controlled.

Brittany's nightmare continued post-op with continued high pressures and fever. Her mother and sister came from California and took turns staying with her and the kids at home. Brittany seemed to take everything in stride and despite how bad she felt, she embraced the loss of her baby, Jessica. On the second post-op day, she made calls to the local funeral home (despite a fever of 103) and arranged for them to pick up her baby. She tearfully said her goodbyes and placed Jessica in the arms of the funeral director herself.

On Thursday, Brittany's doctor announced she could go home the next day if she remained without fever. Ellen, the unit social worker, came to see her to arrange discharge follow-up. "You have had a lot happen to you in the last five days," Ellen said. "Do you feel ready to go home?" Brittany said no.

Brittany worried about having to "jump back into life." At the hospital everyone understood about her suffering; once she got home, she would be "on her own." She was still not feeling well—her leg muscles ached, arms tingled, and chest felt heavy. She didn't understand what had happened and didn't know how to tell her children. Going home was more than she could bear. Ellen talked with her briefly about the effects of grief and finding "safe places and people" to help. She assured her that many parents, especially single mothers, felt very alone and unsure. Ellen gave her some grief-related material to look at when she was ready. Ellen also alerted the nursing staff and asked them to offer Brittany further information about care at home and suggestions about how to talk with her children. The evening nurse promised to talk about the effects of grief when the whole family visited so everyone would be on the same page.

The next day, Brittany's doctor reviewed activity restrictions and medication for home. She encouraged her to call for any reason, even if just to talk. They scheduled her postpartum appointment for the following week and a home visit for the next day. The doctor had read Ellen's carefully documented note and empathized with Brittany's need for safety. When Ellen arrived, Brittany was *able to verbalize grief care and said she thought she "was going to be OK." She was ready to go home.*

Miranda, Brittany's discharge nurse, went over discharge instructions once again, this time so Brittany's mom could hear them. She emphasized over and over to "continue to take good care of yourself; you've been through so much." When it came time to go, she offered Brittany the choice of riding in a wheelchair or walking. Brittany chose to ride, but when she sat in the wheelchair, she began to cry when she remembered holding her other two babies during the ride to the car. Miranda offered her a teddy bear to hold. Brittany gratefully accepted it, hugging the teddy tight as they went out the door.

The next path of the family's journey is discharge. Away from the safety and security of the hospital, the totality of grief sets in as they travel in the "real world," where loss isn't always acknowledged and life doesn't feel the same anymore. The suspension of time encouraged at the hospital comes to a temporary halt; the next few weeks will be filled with appointments, ceremonies and sympathy calls. Their baby will be physically gone, the emptiness filling every crevice. What gifts and supplies can we tuck into to their discharge bag, what words of wisdom can we impart to make it easier? The desire to "fix it" becomes even stronger because we hate to send them unprepared.

Companioning teaches us that families instinctively know what they need. Our humble task is to give them the information and tools to care for themselves, even after they leave us.

The essence of mourning as part of postpartum care

Mourning is the external response to grief. It is how we openly express our feelings of loss. In the environment of compassionate caregivers, Brittany demonstrated courage in the days after delivery. Somehow she knew that life would be different once she got home. Many families in their childbearing years have little exposure to death. Most don't know how to mourn. The world outside the hospital looks pretty scary. Brittany was afraid to face the unknown that was waiting.

Postpartum instruction is more than teaching families how to care for their babies. Any seasoned caregiver will tell you it's more about inspiring and encouraging parents and conveying a "you can do this" philosophy. Grieving families have no baby to tend to, so instead we teach them how to live without and continue loving their little one. That is what mourning is about.

Postpartum teaching

Postpartum teaching to perinatal loss moms can be a challenge. For many of these mothers, attitudes about their bodies have changed. Just a short time ago, they honored their bodies because they were carrying life. Now they may view their bodies as incapable of doing what other women can. As Jeannie, a mother of 22-week twins, put it, "My body let me down. Why should I waste time taking care of it?" But the body must do a lot of work to return to its pre-pregnancy state. The mother needs to continue to care for her body to avoid further complications. One nurse always says, "You've already had enough. Take good care of yourself. You don't need any more bad things happening right now." If possible, postpartum teaching should be done with other family members participating so they can help mother stay on track at home.

Grieving mothers don't remember much about their postpartum instruction. Always utilize and refer to written instructions and physically point out sections in written materials to help jog their memories. If your facility does not have written instructions, hand-write key info on a piece of paper or discharge sheet. Written instructions are an absolute necessity; *no family should go home without them.* Don't forget to include information on:

- Bleeding—what is normal and what is not
- Signs and symptoms of further problems, when to call their provider
- Breast care and the possibility of engorgement, no matter the gestation
- Feelings of depression related to falling levels of hormones and stress
- Birth control, protection against pregnancy until ready physically and emotionally
- Resources—who to call if they are unsure, including names and numbers

The effects of grief

The stress of grief pushes the cardiovascular, hormonal and endocrine system into overtime. Brittany assumed her tingling arms and heavy chest were due to her surgery, but they may have been physical symptoms of grief. All family members can show effects of grief because each has physical and biochemical responses that challenge bodily functions. All family members should be encouraged to care for themselves during this acute time by:

- Eating a balanced diet, avoiding high sugar/high fat foods that create sluggishness.
- Drinking at least eight glasses of fluid a day. Limit caffeinated drinks that interfere with sleep.
- Taking a multivitamin with extra B daily. Mother can continue to take prenatal vitamins or an over-the-counter vitamin with iron.
- Avoiding/limiting alcohol, which might increase feelings of depression.
- Exercising lightly, such as stretching on the floor or walking around the block, which will produce endorphins to relax the body and aid in sleep.
- Resting when possible to overcome effects of insomnia or unusual dreams.
- Allowing help with daily tasks such as cooking, childcare and cleaning. Parents should direct the work and let others know when they need privacy.

EFFECTS OF GRIEF ON THE BODY

- Loss of energy and fatigue
- Changes in sleep habits
- Decreased concentration and forgetfulness
- Weak or achy muscles
- Headaches
- Nausea, diarrhea and/or constipation
- Changes in appetite
- Restlessness, irritability
- Pain or heaviness in the chest
- Shortness of breath
- Dizziness
- Numbness or tingling in arms and legs
- Hot/cold spells
- Changes in sexual desire

- Falling back into usual routines when ready. Caution is given to high detail or technical activities, especially if not sleeping or eating well.
- Expressing feelings as needed. It is OK to talk about the baby, look at photos, etc. if that is comforting.

Talking about depression

All parents worry about depression. The thought of continuing pain and emotional turmoil is more than they can conceptualize. Even before they leave the hospital, they worry they will fall into the black hole of grief and never climb out.

The mother's biochemical state can exacerbate depression. In the weeks following delivery, estrogen and progesterone levels fall to its pre-pregnancy levels. Coupled with acute grief, the combination can be dangerous. Family members try to head off depression for the mother, often insisting on medication and/or intervention. Joe called the support nurse six days after discharge and said, "My wife just stays in the bedroom looking at pictures and crying. She needs something to get her out of this."

Depression should be discussed openly so parents know it is a normal part of grief. As they suspend in grief, they *will* travel deeper into the forest as they gather energy to go forward. One midwife tells her families, "If you weren't depressed, I'd worry about you." Painting a picture of grief/appropriate depression might help.

- Many have problems doing daily activities like getting dressed, cooking, etc. for *at least* two weeks.
- Forgetfulness and lack of energy and enthusiasm are normal for weeks.
- Activities that require thinking, like paying bills, making a grocery list, and doing homework, might be affected for weeks.
- Uncontrolled crying and sadness may come and go for months. Mothers often have a longer bout with sadness than fathers.
- If a parent is unable to get out of bed, refuses to eat or interact with anyone, and/or expresses thoughts of hurting himself or

herself, the doctor should be called immediately. Families should have mental health access information in their post-partum instructions, too.

Learning to live without their baby

How can we begin to help families learn to live without their precious baby? There are no words to explain what is ahead. Some caregivers feel talking about intimate issues of loss is beyond their scope, but the support team can embrace the work together. Families may not be ready to approach hard issues associated with loss at discharge. Subjects can be gently introduced and discussion continued in the following weeks/months:

- *Funerals and ceremonies.* There is no timeframe that must be followed when thinking about post-death rituals. It is important that the family not hurry. The mother needs time to be able to physically participate. Many families aren't sure about having a funeral. They should be encouraged to do what feels right for them while remembering that ceremonies and rituals are a way of showing others how special their baby and part of saying good-bye.

- *Baby items at home.* Saundra's family decided to "get the baby things out of house" after the death of baby Michael. Saundra made them bring it back; she needed to be close to "his things." Parents must decide together what is comforting in regards to baby items and direct family and friends as needed. Removing baby's things from the home does not remove the pain associated with them.

- *Finding answers.* When the fogginess lifts, the "why" question will surface. It is important that post-mortem studies be discussed on multiple occasions and framed in the context of trying to find answers, especially for future pregnancies. One support nurse terms post-mortem studies as "a lasting gift your baby can give to you and your future children." If families are still unsure, suggest alternatives such as placental exams, chromosome testing, cultures, etc. Like John and Mindy in the first story, many families decline autopsy not realizing the drive they may later have for answers.

- *Learning to grieve and mourn.* Parents are often on the same plane initially but soon develop their own style of coping. Their mourning can be misinterpreted by their partner: "He didn't feel the same about the baby as I did." Differences may be attributed to gender (i.e. men and women cope differently) but sometimes the differences stem from partnership issues. Penny and Carol wanted to have a baby together for six years. When their baby, Adam, died before birth, each took on a unique role in mourning. Carol was "the strong one," taking care of the household and decisions while Penny retreated in grief for weeks. Months later, Carol experienced weeks of crying and depression. Supportive partners balance each other. Both parents in the family can't be overwhelmed with grief, so one usually (and subconsciously) puts acute grief aside so the family can stay functional. In most families that is usually the male partner. It is vital that families understand that all members of the family must mourn in their own way.

- *Creating new support systems.* Some parents find that previous support systems don't fit in their current situation. Family should be given ideas about how to create new supports to walk with them in their grief. At discharge, the thought of reaching out to strangers might be uncomfortable; giving them permission to connect when they are ready offers alternatives and choices.

Most of all, families need encouragement to believe in their ability to survive this painful journey. A "go with your gut" philosophy should guide them in the initial days and weeks. The best gift caregivers can give before discharge is passing the torch of intuition and instinct. "You know what is right for you deep down inside," one physician tells her patients. "Follow your heart, even if others are telling you something else. Take your time and allow yourself space to heal."

THE UNIQUENESS OF GRIEF
How different family members react

Mother
- Typically more intense in her acute grief; displays more emotion
- Grief is impacted by physiological changes in her body and hormone levels
- May feel a deeper attachment to the baby, especially in early months of pregnancy
- May feel more openly responsible for loss

Father
- Grief may be more controlled, less visible signs; may feel a need to be "strong"
- Often returns to work/usual routine more quickly
- Intense need to "take care of her"
- Level of attachment to baby, prior to delivery, more abstract
- May have more long-term effects from loss

Grandparents
- Often grieve twice—for their grandchild and for their child
- May have history of own perinatal loss that was unsupported
- May be unsure of how to support their child as an adult, unsure of how to help

Siblings
- Age & development of child will directly affect the outward expressions of grief; expressions are often misinterpreted at home, at school, at play
- Most adults underestimate a child's ability to grieve
- Children can grieve over temporary changes in relationships with parents and changes in the household as well as a lost sibling
- Play is a creative outlet of grief

One final moment

The minute the family leaves the unit, there may be no more opportunities to touch and see their precious baby. Families may need one final moment with their baby, one last chance to soak up any remaining memories. Offering time for final moments should be a part of discharge support. We offer the opportunity and invite them to create their last goodbyes:

- Would you like some private time with your baby before you go?
- Would you like to help prepare the body for the funeral home?
- Would you like more pictures? A last blessing or prayer?
- Is there anything you hoped to have that hasn't been done yet?

Parents will remember their last moments in detail. Deanna and Travis were guided by their nurse in their last moments of good-bye. They had decided to "let him go" eight hours after death for autopsy. (They were afraid waiting would affect the results.) With the nurse's help, they gently undressed and wrapped him, kissing his tiny cheeks before the last fold of cloth covered his face. They escorted him down to the holding area where the transporter was waiting. As Deanna handed him over, she said, "Take good care of my baby." The parents, nurse and transporter were all in tears. Deanna told her support caregiver months later, "That was the hardest thing I have ever done, but to get him ready was the right thing for me to do."

What about parents who did not see their baby after death? How can we help them in the final minutes of their hospital stay? Deborah and Rico chose not to see their baby after delivery. They had been told of Misty's severe birth defects and decided before delivery not to see her. After their discharge was completed, Deborah's nurse said, "I know that it was a tough decision not to spend time with Misty. Some parents tell us how hard it is down the road when they didn't see or touch their baby. This will be your last chance. I'm going to leave you alone for a few minutes. If you still don't want to see her when I come back, that will be the best decision for you." When the nurse returned, Deborah and

Rico asked to see little Misty. They spent an additional two hours at the hospital saying hello and goodbye. Sometimes the last moment makes a difference.

Going out the door

When the bags are packed and papers signed, it is time for the final ride out of the hospital. The last bit of hope has dissolved and the dream is over. They are going home without their baby. For many families, this is the hardest part. Discharge routines should be adapted to meet the family's current state:

- We usually escort all our families to the door. Is that OK with you?
- Mothers usually ride in a wheelchair. Would you like to ride or would you rather walk?
- We usually dismiss our patients at the front door. Would you prefer a quieter place?

There is no greater emptiness than a mother's arms at discharge. As one mother said, "It hurt so much to leave the hospital with only my purse in my lap. I'll never forget the feeling." Termed the "empty arms syndrome," the will to cling to something is powerful; many mothers gladly accept a teddy bear or their baby's blanket/Memory Keeper to hold. The ride from the unit to the hospital exit can be emotional. It is important that the transporter be aware of the situation (if non-unit personnel are utilized). If possible, a caregiver who has been directly involved with the family should escort them to their car. Their last moments at the hospital should feel safe and comforting.

Letting them go

It's hard to know if we have given the family the tools they need to survive the next few weeks. Once they are gone, we wonder if we did enough, said the right words, offered life-sustaining encouragement. Yet if we companioned them, we gave them what they needed as we walked alongside. It is still their grief to own and experience; it was our privilege (and challenge) to be part of it.

CHAPTER EIGHT

OTHER PREGNANCY LOSSES: SUPPORT WHEN THERE IS "NO BABY"

This is Rosa's story, a tribute to a tiny baby.

Rosa was transported to the nearest emergency room after her husband, Greg, found her doubled over in the bathroom. Within minutes, an ultrasound confirmed an ectopic pregnancy and ruptured fallopian tube. Surgery was done immediately; they were able to save Rosa but not her tube—or, of course, the baby.

As Rosa recuperated on the surgical unit, she tried to sort out the events of the last two days, despite her Demerol-induced haze. Her heart warmed as she remembered the utter excitement about the pregnancy. She and Greg had danced around the house when the plus sign appeared on the pregnancy test stick. It had been the happiest day of her life! Something was growing inside her. She was sure their baby would be the smartest, funniest, most handsome and talented person in the world. Since the pain-filled moment in the bathroom, the utter joy had been replaced by terror. In the blur of the emergency room, she clearly heard the doctor's words: immediate surgery or possible death. Her thoughts drifted, wanting to go back to when life seemed perfect. Where did it all go? "Where is the baby?" she sleepily asked Greg. He dismissed her question and told her to rest.

When the social worker stopped by, Rosa asked, "Do you know where my baby went after surgery?" Taken aback by the question, she suggested Rosa ask the doctor. The next day, Kelly's doctor carefully explained that at six weeks gestation, "the baby" wasn't more than a tiny cluster of cells hardly visible to the naked eye. There wasn't really a baby to find during the surgery. Rosa knew that a baby was small in the beginning, but only a cluster of cells? In her mind, the baby was a miniature newborn, complete with Greg's characteristic smile.

Family and friends came to visit and focused on her physical recovery. No one ever mentioned the pregnancy. Rosa told herself they were right. It was silly to pine away for a tiny cluster of cells. She had only known about the pregnancy for a few short weeks, hardly time to get attached. Yet, there was still something lingering, something unsettling, something unfinished.

When Caroline, a coworker, came to visit, she asked, "How are you really?" Caroline had experienced an early miscarriage a few years before. "I still mourn over that baby," she told Rosa. "They told me I had to have a D & C to stop the bleeding; I wanted them to save the baby but they said they couldn't. I know I wasn't pregnant very long, but I had big plans for that little one." Rosa mustered up her courage and asked, "Do you know where your baby went?" "Sure," said Caroline. "The hospital has a special cremation program for early babies. Bill and I attended the service when they spread the ashes in the hospital garden." Rosa pictured her cute little baby again. "How would I find out where my baby is?" she asked.

Caroline offered to connect her with a support nurse at the hospital. The nurse came the next day and they talked for over an hour. She helped Rosa feel OK about mourning over her unfinished—but still loved—baby. Rosa and Greg attended the pregnancy loss support group the next week. On the way home, they began to talk about how they *both felt about the pregnancy. It was the start of many conversations to come.*

On a blustery fall day, Rosa, Greg, and their families held a remembrance service in the church courtyard. It was the day the baby would have been due. Their priest blessed the couple and offered words of healing. They left a tiny angel statue in the flowerbed, in memory of their first baby. He or she may not have been more than a tiny cluster of cells, but today he or she was much more: cherished and loved.

First trimester miscarriage, blighted ovum, ectopic pregnancy and molar pregnancy: when a baby is a tiny embryo, a beginning life disguised as a cluster of cells, can someone mourn its passing?

It is often hard for caregivers to appreciate the depth of pain early pregnancy loss can bring. Parents often experience a multitude of reactions; what is devastating to one family may be only physically uncomfortable to another. There is nothing to touch, no photos to take, no footprints to do. We, too, may be unsure how to proceed. As we companion families in early loss, the art of honoring grief takes on a new dimension. It is our mission to find a way to walk alongside and witness their story in whatever form it comes.

A special beginning and ending

In the first few weeks of pregnancy, the mother's and father's lives are a whirlwind of emotion. Anticipation and excitement couple with uncertainty and doubt. Am I ready for this? Will everything be OK? What will the next months be like? Life changes with the advent of a positive pregnancy test. Parents announce to the world they are going to have a baby! At first, it seems unreal or too abstract to comprehend. Parents often start the journey in low gear, concentrating more on the pregnancy. In the beginning

TYPES OF EARLY PREGNANCY LOSS

Miscarriage
Delivery of an embryo or fetus less than 20 weeks gestation
that shows no evidence of life once outside the mother.

Ectopic pregnancy (also known as a tubal pregnancy)
Implantation of a fertilized egg somewhere other than the
lining of the uterus, usually the fallopian tube. Embryo
cannot develop and, if the tube ruptures, can be fatal to the
mother.

Blighted ovum (anembryonic pregnancy)
A form of very early miscarriage. No embryo forms inside
gestational sac.

Molar pregnancy (also termed hydatiform mole)
Fertilized egg grows abnormally into a mass of tissue rather
than an embryo and/or placenta. Can be complete or partial.
Causes excessive uterine bleeding and may lead to uterine
(trophoblastic) cancer.

months, pregnancy is more about lofty hopes and visions, something yet to be.

Rosa and Greg literally danced for joy when the pregnancy was confirmed. They reveled in the new life a baby would bring. Two weeks later, the flutter of excitement left as quickly as it came. In the emergency room, they became suspended between what was supposed to be and what will never come. Like a runner who prepares for the race but never makes it to the starting line, their dreams were built on hopes never fulfilled.

Not every parent grieves the passing of an early pregnancy. Tammy went to the emergency room when she began bleeding. She knew she was pregnant but hadn't found the time between school and work to make a prenatal appointment. When the doctor told her she was miscarrying, she wasn't surprised. At her follow-up appointment, she told her midwife, "To be honest, I was relieved. I wasn't ready to be pregnant and I hadn't thought about it being a baby yet. Maybe someday I'll be sad, but I'm OK right now."

Each parent builds and shapes their relationship with the tiny embryo. For some, it is automatic; for others, it comes in time. Since grief is an outcome of love, the kind of journey a parent creates will be molded by the level of commitment to the pregnancy. The path will be different for each one.

Sometimes it's about more than the baby

In the crisis of the moment, among the rush of bleeding and intense pain, the focus of early pregnancy loss often changes: mother comes first, baby second. When Greg heard the words "life-threatening," he only thought about his wife. The baby, all he had thought about up to that time, was pushed back in his mind. He concentrated on the here-and-now and Rosa. For days after, he stayed with her, afraid something else might happen. At support group, Greg talked about that day. "You think life couldn't be grander until some stranger tells you the most precious person in the world might die. It was like someone slapped me across the face. I never knew pregnancy could be life-threatening." Rosa

WHEN A MOTHER DIES

Sometimes mothers die, too. Fortunately, maternal death happens infrequently, especially in our world of modern medicine. Many OB caregivers today have never experienced an adult death unless they have prior non-obstetrics experience. When it happens, the whole unit is stunned, unsure what to do next.

There are no words of preparation, no protocols to ease the shock of a maternal death in OB. We hope you will never experience it, but if you do:

- Reach out to another unit in the hospital that experiences frequent death, such as ICU. They can provide direction such as hospital protocols, coroner criteria, death paperwork, etc.
- Utilize the same principles in supporting the family—offering time, information, and support. Access any available support systems in the hospital to help.
- If possible, keep mother and baby together or nearby. Avoid moving mother to another area or bring her body back to OB. Families may need time together.
- The concept of mementos can be adapted for mothers, too. Photos of mother and baby together, handprints together, etc. can be a wonderful gift for the family.

didn't remember the events exactly like Greg. She said, "I heard the doctor but didn't really think about the possibility of dying until it was all over. I remember feeling bad the baby had to die because of me."

The effects of threatened mortality can last for months. Wanda miscarried at home; three days later she hemorrhaged and had to have an emergency D & C. "Frankly I thought the miscarriage wasn't a big deal until I was rushed to the hospital. I was scared out of my mind! It was all I could think about for weeks. What would have happened to my other kids if I had died?" Mothers with molar pregnancies have worries for years. "When they told me about the risk of cancer, I flipped out!" said Marian, a woman who thought she had "a late miscarriage" until the path report diagnosed a hydatiform mole. "I went from wondering about a new baby to worrying about cancer in one week. It was too much to think about." Personal issues of mortality may be a mountain to summit before coming to the grief journey of an early baby.

The "Was there ever a baby?" question

Most of us equate pregnancy with the beginning of a baby. When a malfunction in conception creates a blighted ovum or molar pregnancy, parents often struggle with the question "Was there ever a baby?" For weeks, Donnita celebrated the beginning of her first pregnancy. After the ultrasound she was told "there was no baby in the sac. "She wondered for weeks if there ever was a baby but was afraid to ask. After Keisha's miscarriage, she decided to bury the baby. Before the arrangements were complete, her doctor called and told her what she passed was a molar pregnancy. She contacted the bereavement nurse for advice about what to do next. "Is there a baby to bury or was it just a tumor?" she asked. It is hard enough when baby is so tiny that it can't be seen. For parents who aren't sure there was ever a baby, grief becomes more confusing. In Keisha's words, they don't know if they have "a reason to grieve."

THE "HARD PARTS" ABOUT EARLY
PERINATAL LOSS

* *Confusion*: Was it a "real" pregnancy? Was it really "a baby?"

* *Physical issues*: Severe pain, bleeding and possible surgery may color the experience. If left untreated (especially in ectopic pregnancy), can lead to maternal death.

* *Emptiness*: Nothing to see or hold, no tangible memories. Often the gender of the baby is not known.

* *Multiple losses*: Many struggle with loss of pregnancy as much as death of baby.

* *Lingering questions*: Many times there are no definitive answers as to why a pregnancy ends in the first trimester.

* *Incongruent grief*: Mothers and fathers grieve differently for an early loss.

* *General lack of support*: From friends and family and society in general. At the hospital, may be in a non-OB area/have limited access to perinatal loss support.

* *Impact on future pregnancies*: Many miscarriages are caused by chromosomal issues; ectopic pregnancies can affect future fertility; molar pregnancies can lead to uterine cancer; all affect the parents' decisions about trying again.

The size of grief

It is easy to dismiss the grief when there is nothing to see or touch. The magnitude of grief can be powerful as we hold a stillborn baby in our arms. However, a D & C canister or a pathology container does not evoke those same kinds of feelings. Many caregivers make the unconscious assumption that grief correlates to the size of the baby or length of the pregnancy. Yet, the size of the baby doesn't matter. Grief depends on the size of the pain parents feel.

Estrella came to the outpatient center for a D & C. Through her translator, she told the pre-op nurse that she had named the baby and would like a priest to bless him after the procedure. In the quiet of the recovery room, Estrella and her family laid hands on the pathology container as the hospital priest led them in prayer. Unconventional by most recovery room standards, it was what Estrella and Rico needed in their healing. Their baby may have been not visible and whole in the container, but he was still wanted and loved.

Finding ways to honor and witness their grief

How can we begin to honor the spirit of families experiencing early pregnancy loss? In the emergency room, triage area or recovery suite, there is so little time to explore the intimate concepts of grief. Within the cloud of medications and anesthesia, how can parents lead us? How will we know what they need?

Our time with the patient may be more limited and our care more concentrated, but our goal remains the same: offering the family the most positive experience possible after the loss of their pregnancy. Companioning teaches us to:

• Provide physical care to the mother and support to her whole family.
• Offer a safe and respectful environment in which grief can be expressed if they choose.
• Create moments where the life of their baby can be explored and possibly mourned.

- Gently lead family, giving them information so they can make choices that will be healing for them.

The foundation to early pregnancy loss support lies in the caregiver's ability to enter into the family's story. Many mothers find they are miscarrying just hours or days after the pregnancy is confirmed; the shock of the news along with physical discomfort impairs their ability to relay what they need. We must search through the pain of the experience until we are able to understand. Caregivers must:

Leave personal feelings about early pregnancy loss at the door. Some caregivers have definite opinions about when life begins. Judy, a recovery room nurse, believed life was sacred from the moment of conception. It upset her when mothers declined information about the hospital burial program; she felt all families would want to honor their unborn babies. Judy had to keep her personal feelings aside in order to meet families where they were.

Become curious. Asking questions such as "Has finding out about what happened with your pregnancy been hard for you?" can open a conversation that leads to understanding. Simply asking questions as you provide physical care—such as "How long have you known you were pregnant?" and "Were you excited when you found out?"—can invite the mother and father to tell their story.

Respect and honor the numbness of crisis. Many early pregnancy loss parents are overwhelmed and unsure how to react. Our words and actions can open the door for later mourning. Ebony, an ER chaplain, visits all miscarrying mothers. She tells them, "Every woman feels a little different about pregnancy loss. Some struggle, some don't. So much has happened in the last few hours, you might not know how you feel. When the shock wears off, how you feel is right for you." She gives them a packet about grief; she tells them if they are not interested in reading it, maybe they will have a friend who could benefit from it. Ebony finds most mothers read the information once they are in the safety of their homes.

Ease the fear to help in the work of mourning. Extended family are often overwhelmed as they sit helpless by. Fathers especially struggle as they are thrown into making decisions about their partner as well as their baby. Providing a supportive environment and assurances that the mother is being well cared for will ease the fear and pain the family experiences. It is often helpful if one member of the team can concentrate on the father and his well-being. He may need extra TLC to cope with what is going on.

Be available. Physical presence and expressions of empathy must be even more purposeful because of the limited time at the bedside. Becca told her support group she would never forget the resident doctor who helped her. "She told me she was sorry I lost the baby and she hardly ever left me alone. She must have known I was afraid." The whole team—doctor, midwife, chaplain, social worker, emergency room and surgical suite staff—come together to create a powerful presence.

Creating memories

Parents say one of the hardest parts about losing a baby in the early weeks of pregnancy is not having anything tangible to give comfort or validate the beginning life. For those who mourn the tiny baby's passing, there is nothing to hold onto.

As their companions, we can offer gifts of experience and creativity. We can empower the family to envision their tiny baby and explore memories that will sustain them. Parents can find healing ways to honor the spirit of their hoped-for baby with direction and encouragement during the acute experience and after by:

Giving their baby a name: A name solidifies the baby's presence in the world. For early babies, choosing a name can be difficult since the sex of the baby isn't known. Families can "go with their gut" and select a name they had been thinking about or choose a name that would be appropriate for either a boy or girl. There are no time limits on when a name can be chosen; families can name their early baby whenever it is healing for them. Vanessa, a nurse on the postpartum unit, suffered a miscarriage 20 years ago. At

GENDER-NEUTRAL NAMES FOR WHEN A BABY IS BORN EARLY

Morgan	Shelby
Riley	Michael
Billie	Bobbie
Jackie	Kelsey
Chris	McKenzie
Taylor	Jordan
Corey	Adrian
Jodie	Tracy
Reagan	Whitney
Angel	Jessie

the time, her doctor told her "to move on." At a bereavement conference, thoughts about that baby came rushing back and she felt she needed to honor the baby from long ago. With the help of a friend, she chose a name (Justin) and bought a birthstone angel in the hotel gift shop in his honor.

Having a ceremony for the baby: Rituals and ceremonies are a lasting way to remember loved ones. A blessing or prayer ceremony can be offered at the bedside or hospital chapel or families can create their own ceremony at home. Greg and Rosa decided to wait until their due date to have a ceremony; others may have a tree planting or balloon release soon after their loss. Virginia, a grandmother of two miscarried babies, lights a candle every year on "their special day." Ceremonies don't have to be formal or ornate, they only need to come from the heart.

Making a special memory packet: Parents can still collect mementos for their baby if they choose. Some hospitals provide the beginnings of a Memory Keeper for early pregnancy loss families along with suggestions of items to add. Typically these Keepers are small, soft-sided folders or boxes, just big enough to hold an ultrasound picture, ceramic heart, flower, etc. It is not the contents of the Memory Keeper that touch the family's heart; it is the caregiver's acknowledgment that their baby deserved a holder for memories.

Deciding about disposition: If parents viewed the loss as a death of their baby, they may want to explore options of disposition—how the baby is "laid to rest." Some families choose to have a private disposition (i.e., burial or cremation) despite the fact their baby's remains fit inside a urine cup. Unless asked, most do not express any disposition requests; they don't often even realize there is an option until long after the loss. Many hospitals are creating special disposition programs where products of conception are communally cremated or buried (rather than incinerated with other surgical specimens). Families often find comfort in knowing their baby was treated with dignity and respect and has a "final resting place." As with other support systems, families need information and time to sort out decisions in order to find what is best for them.

Preparing for the deep divide of grief

Before leaving the facility, early pregnancy loss parents need information for home. Discharge instructions should include basic information about early pregnancy loss, how to care for mother's body at home, and sexual intercourse/birth control guidelines. They should also have phone numbers of support people they can access in the weeks and months after. Some hospitals have systems in place that automatically refer patients to support programs. Parents may need those vital connections. They will appreciate written and verbal information that helps them cope with the ups and downs of early pregnancy loss.

- *Mothers and fathers often feel differently about pregnancy loss at first.* Mothers have physical symptoms and may feel a deeper sense of loss. Fathers, with a different level of investment at this point in the pregnancy, may be more concerned about their partner and less about the baby. It is important to talk about each other's feelings and respect each other's grief.

- *Family and friends who have been supportive in the past may have difficulty understanding the loss.* Parents may find it necessary to reach out to new supports and forgive those who don't know how to honor their grief. "My mother tried to help in those first few weeks after the miscarriage," a mother in support group said, "but she'd say things like 'you can get pregnant again' or 'at least you weren't very far along.' She didn't know her comments were hurtful."

- *Because early pregnancy loss is full of mixed feelings, the next weeks and months can be filled with surprising and conflicting emotions.* Parents need to remember to take care of themselves as individuals and as a couple.

When it is difficult to walk alongside

In the confusing world of early pregnancy loss, it is hard to be a companion. There is so little time to explore their story and there are so many stories to hear. We can only listen with our hearts as we witness their experience. We can inform and comfort, encourage and inspire. As their companions, we will do our best to be a part of their life-impacting experience.

CHAPTER NINE

AFTER DISCHARGE: CONTINUING COMPANIONING

Dear Katie,

I found one of your cards in a drawer today and thought of you. Can you believe it's been three years since Brandon passed away?

Sometimes it seems like it happened to someone else, a crushing part of a movie or an ugly newscast. Other times, I still feel the pain like yesterday. When it comes back, it's not quite so devastating and there are parts I can actually smile about. He looked so peaceful as you handed him to me—he was beautiful, wasn't he? Mike and I couldn't have done it without you...just walking into our room helped us to be stronger, braver. You helped us love our baby when we were afraid. (Hard to believe you could be afraid of your own baby.) What a blessing you were.

You've been a lifesaver since, too. A gentle voice on the other end of the phone when everyone else had forgotten. And the Mother's Day card touched me more than you can know—it was the only acknowledgment I got that day. How would I have made it without you? You gave me permission to remember and love him when everyone else said move on.

We have a new baby! His name is Blake and he is a spitting image of Mike right down to the dimples! How we love him! Every day he fills my heart with joy. Sometimes I wonder if Brandon would have looked like him or laughed like him. It's weird how you can get filled up and empty at the same time.

I'm afraid I wasn't very appreciative of all you did for Mike and me back then. Now that time has done some healing, I want to thank you from the bottom of my heart. Please know you will always be a very special part of our family.

Yours,
Jenna

A marathon runner prepares for months for the long race. He starts slowly, building strength and endurance for the long haul ahead. The long road of grief is like a marathon, but bereaved parents have no training regime to support them. They travel through the weeks and months after their loss fueled by some unknown force, putting one foot in front of the other, living one day at a time. There are no rest stops and no finish line; they keep running, hoping for ways to feel whole again.

More than ever, perinatal loss families need someone to continue walking alongside them in their journey, someone who experienced the life-changing beginning and understands. Although they are not physically in our care, we still can companion them. The aftercare we provide is often a lifeline in a world where an empty rocking chair is a heart-wrenching symbol of their lives.

Filling a void

Jenna and Mike opted for an underwater delivery in their hospital's birthing center. Minutes after delivery, doctors were attending to their baby's lifeless body. Hours later, Jenna and Mike were told Brandon had severe heart and lung defects. Their precious baby died in their arms a few hours later.

Katie was Jenna's nurse during Brandon's ten-hour life. She was new to OB, transferring from the cancer unit a few months prior. Feeling totally out of her element, she "flew by the seat of her pants" as she helped them say goodbye to their son. As they readied to go home the next day, she asked if she could "stay in touch." She remembered how families of cancer patients came back to the unit after their loved one died; they taught her about the lasting connection between families and caregivers. Over the next year, Katie would occasionally call or send notes. They would chat about Brandon or life in general. When the letter that opens this chapter came years later, Katie was stunned because she felt she hadn't done much—called a few times, sent a card or two. But to Jenna, Katie was the person who helped her maneuver the void between the security of the hospital and the emptiness of home.

When we walk alongside

During the time of delivery and death, we were an intimate part of the family's experience. After they leave the hospital, they are trudging on without us. We want to help, but the geographical distance is intimidating. We want to pull them back and tuck them under our wing. The wanting to fix, to be responsible for finding a way out of the dark wilderness, rises again.

The foundation of companioning reminds us that it is not our mission to treat their grief. Rather, it is our privilege to continue providing presence and light where we can. Aftercare, whether it flows from an organized program or the caring of one individual, offers a safe and secure place that says "your grief is honored here." Our aftercare also helps them collect tools for survival and offers respite from the rest of the world. We still can't fix it but we can be there for them. Our gift is so powerful, we will never know how much it means to them.

The essence of aftercare is simple: it provides a personal connection to people who are willing to travel the grief journey with them. In the months following perinatal loss, aftercare can:

- Offer time with professional and lay support people who honor the spirit of grieving families and believe in their ability to survive their loss.
- Help sort through the disorder and confusion of grief and assure a sense of normalcy in their crazy world.
- Create opportunities to continue telling their story as they become a part of a support community with other parents.

Tonya, the mother of Jacey, who died in NICU at four months of age, said the support she received the following year was a "lifesaver"—the only way she could have survived. When families make comments like Tonya's, it is easy to buy into the notion that our care "saves" them. Aftercare is not about our accomplishments. Instead, it is a flow of compassion, one that gives the family courage to explore their own grief and grow into a new normal. The families are the real heroes. We merely have the privilege to watch it happen.

Exploring the work of mourning

When the shock of the initial loss wears away, parents often ache for something to fill the emptiness. They reside in a place they have never been and don't know how to begin. In a world where extended family, friends, coworkers, and neighbors have moved past the moment, parents flounder at how to be functioning people again. Well-intended people encourage them to put the experience behind them: "you're young, you'll have another baby; "it was God's will;" "your other children need you." Parents float in a sea of grief, unsure which direction to swim. They want to make sense of it all, find some meaning in the pain. Telling their story is a part of the process. They yearn for others to hear. They need to ask why over and over until they realize there are no answers. They need to find ways to show others how life-changing their baby was.

As companions, we know that each member of the family must travel their own grief journey. Each will need different tools on their unique path to healing. We offer our experience and a variety of supports so families can pick and choose what feels right for them. The "go with your gut" philosophy applies; as caregivers, we help families sort out options so they pursue ones that feel right. We invite them to create their own journey, trying different venues until they hit on one that works for them. Many aftercare programs include:

People who are willing to listen. Many parents find they have little opportunity in their own community to talk about their baby and their grief. When families know there is someone a phone call or e-mail away, the feelings of loneliness and isolation diminish. Christa "lost it" when the second coworker of the day reminded her that many miscarried babies have genetic problems. She called her support nurse on her lunch hour, needing someone to validate her anger.

Reading materials about grief. For some, reading about grief puts words to feelings. "When I read how that one mother felt guilty, I realized that's how I felt. I couldn't explain it until then." Books can be purchased or borrowed from the public library or hospital's lending library. Many families aren't sure how to find books at first. It helps to have suggestions to start.

Expression through writing. Journaling can be intimidating, especially for those who haven't tried it in the past. One social worker keeps inexpensive journals in her office with writing suggestions pasted inside. "I never wrote anything in my life," said one mother, "until my pastor encouraged me to start a journal. I've told it everything. Sometimes when I'm blue, I reread the pages and I see that I'm stronger than before."

Opportunities to participate in ongoing events such as memorial services, burial of the ashes, scrapbooking workshops, remembrance walks, etc. Events can provide comfort and solace after others have forgotten; they can also give the family a reason to come back to the place where their baby lived and died. Julie, an aunt of little Lenny, who died 15 years ago, participates in the hospital's annual Walk to Remember each year. "It's Lenny's only day," she explains, "We do this together; it's all we have."

Invitations to join a community of grieving parents. There is something special about the connection among grieving parents. As one mother put it, "It's like joining an exclusive club, one under any other circumstances you wouldn't consider, but because of what happened, it's the only place to be." Parents are drawn together. They meet through a friend, a chat room on the internet or a support group. Whether it is one-on-one or a group setting, a community of grieving parents creates energy through shared pain and growth. Parents can talk to other grieving parents without judgment. A community of grieving parents becomes the measure of normalcy. "I figured I had to be the strong one all the time," TC explained after his first support group meeting, "then I saw that guy break down in front of his girlfriend. I guess it's OK if I fall apart sometimes."

DIMENSIONS OF AFTERCARE
How we can stay connected

Face-to-face visits, either in the hospital or community setting
Physical presence provides comfort in the midst of chaos.

Phone calls
The sound of a voice reconnects.

E-mail
This is an easy way for many families and can be done at times that suit them best.

Internet bulletin boards or chat groups
Connects families in the privacy of their homes.

Written notes and cards
Can be saved and reread.

Newsletters
A great way to distribute inspirational messages and information.

Support groups
Parents helping parents.

Memorial events
Continue to acknowledge the presence of their baby in their family.

Workshops related to grief issues
Combines support and learning.

Service-related projects
Helping others together can be healing.

Support during the low times of grief. Parents will have periods where the pain of loss returns with a vengeance. Griefbursts—sudden, unexpected periods of sadness—are usually triggered by some event or experience. It may be an upcoming holiday or some sensual memory. "It sneaks up on you," Patty told her support caregiver. "You think, 'I'm getting better,' then boom! It hits you like a box of rocks." Birthdays, death anniversaries, due dates, etc. can be very intense for families, especially if they are not acknowledged by those around them. One program sends a Mother's Day card to their newly bereaved mothers. Like Jenna, Sherilynn experienced the same feeling about Mother's Day: "Do you know you were the only one who considered me a mother that day? Thank you for that."

Staying connected in the long months of grief

Companioning can raise the bar in aftercare, letting families lead and direct the kind of support offered. If we continue to listen with our hearts and let families lead us, our care moves beyond the standard follow-up and into a synchronous flow of compassion.

Families tell us they appreciate our connection. A call, voicemail message or thinking-of-you card is a gesture of caring that fuels families to keep going, to attend to their own grief while taking care of themselves. Our aftercare helps families:

• *Concentrate on their physical care*. Parents need gentle reminders of a healthy lifestyle in order to cope with the physical effects of grief.

• *Talk about their labor experience and baby*. Parents can always tell their story to us because we know how sacred it is.

• *Discuss hurtful comments from well-meaning people*. Parents often need someone to sort out their relationships with others, especially those they perceive as unsupportive or uncaring.

• *Process feelings with someone besides their significant other*. Parents often process their grief and pain differently. Partners

CRITICAL TIMES IN THE JOURNEY
When grieving families need companioning the most

1st week after loss—to assure their physical safety and comfort

4-6 weeks—a time when mothers seem to be at their lowest

3-4 months—when life is supposed to be back to normal; also a time when some couples consider another pregnancy

Due dates and birth/death dates—baby's special days; others may not remember

Holidays—family-oriented times that often bring griefbursts; Mother's and Father's Day may be especially difficult for parents with no surviving children in the home

Subsequent pregnancies—a resurgence of fear and emotion; will it happen again?

may need other outlets for grief. As one mother said, "I feel I'm always bringing him down when he's trying to stay up. But I still need to talk about her. I'm not ready to let go."

- *Explore ways to memorialize their baby.* Parents often want to continue to remember their baby and can benefit from suggestions.

- *Support for whole family.* Parents find they must support their family's grief, especially the grief of their other children. They look to their caregivers for direction.

- *Considering new kinds of supports.* People who have been supportive in the past might not be comfortable in grief; parents may have to reach out and create new supports. "My sister will always be my best friend," Jessica said, "but right now, she doesn't get it and I don't have the strength to show her. I need someone else."

- *A general lifting up as they build a new normal.* Learning to live without their baby can be hard work. Parents often need someone to inspire them to keep going. Sarah felt better when her caregiver told her how much he admired her courage and conviction. "I needed that," she wrote in her journal.

Connecting by phone

At 3-6 weeks following the loss, the world seems to return to life as it was before, leaving parents behind. A phone call can be a welcome opportunity to retell the story and seek comfort. Phone communication challenges our companioning skills; we do not have the benefit of all our senses to hear the person and understand. Our sense of intuition must be fully enabled if we are to listen with our hearts. When companioning via the phone:

- *Be prepared.* Have information at hand such as names of children, date of loss, etc.

- *Assure a proper environment for listening.* Noise and activity will distract the parent and the listener. Make sure your total focus can be directed at them.

DIFFERENT KINDS OF SUPPORT GROUPS
   FOR FAMILIES

- *A closed group* has a specific number of sessions, usually 6-8 weeks; there is a set agenda to help move through grief. Some families appreciate the defined period and the relationships formed by the consistent membership.

- *An open group* is an ongoing group where members come and go as they need. Some families attend only one or two sessions; others attend off and on for years. Betty started coming to group after the death of her grandson, James. At first, she came "for her daughter" but stayed even after her daughter stopped coming. "The group got Shelley through. There is a special place in my heart for it. The people come and go but the feelings in the room are the same. If I can be a part of that in any way, I will."

- *An internet-driven group*, often called a chatroom, pulls people from a large geographical space. Members are anonymous (although many choose to share their identity through private e-mail). Families can participate on their own timeframes. Cindy belongs to three different chatrooms. "If I can't sleep in the middle of the night, I can always find someone to talk to in a chatroom." Some grieving parents opt for the flexibility and anonymity of cyberspace over the personal face-to-face of a local support group.

- *Develop an opening that feels right for you.* Identify yourself and the purpose of the call in a concise, caring manner. Your objective is to make the person on the other end of the line as comfortable as possible.

- *Ask questions that will encourage conversation:* Even simple questions such as "What is the hardest part for you right now?" will open doors of understanding.

- *End the call on a positive note.* Review what was discussed and include affirmations of their personal growth. Parents will feel rejuvenated and reenergized with your comments.

- *Follow up after the call.* A written note or card can reinforce principles and help continue relationships. Example: "Thank you for sharing your story with me today. I feel privileged to be part of your experience. Don't forget to continue taking good care of yourself. Grief is such hard work!"

Joining groups: a community of support

It has been said that misery loves company. Being with other families who understand and sympathize can be comforting, especially to newly grieving parents. A peer support group meeting can provide an environment in which grieving parents can talk about their baby as much they need, explore feelings of grief, and gain suggestions in dealing with loss in their everyday life. There is something about speaking the words out loud that validates their feelings and provides an indescribable release. As thoughts and feelings flow, powerful connections form among parents. They literally and figuratively hold each other up. For many, it is the only lifeline they have.

About ten percent of families reach out for peer support. Some choose to find support in other venues, such as their church, friends or family. Some feel a group setting is too overwhelming. Some cannot muster the energy to come to the hospital. For those who do attend, the support group is a coming together of souls in the wilderness. Together, they hack away at the darkness, hoping to find some light.

Some groups are situation-focused, such as an early pregnancy loss group or a subsequent pregnancy group. Some smaller communities might facilitate groups with a larger population of grief, such as parents who have lost a child at any age. A group facilitator offers physical and emotional comfort and assures the meeting is a safe and sacred place to share feelings and stories.

Regardless of the experience, parents come together to find a way to heal their broken hearts. They seek what they need, listening to others and asking questions. The weight of their pain lifts as they realize they "aren't crazy after all." The community of parents helps them see they aren't alone and gives them energy to move through their grief. As one long-time group member said, "I walked out of the first meeting and said to myself 'Thank God! I'm not losing my mind after all!' Those people felt just like I did. It gave me what I needed to go another day."

Continuing the memories

As hospital caregivers, we are the keepers of leftover memories. The flames of tiny baby spirits live within our walls. Many parents find warmth when they return for an in-hospital support group or remembrance event. They know that no matter what happens on the outside, their baby will be remembered here. Yet, the fear of coming back makes them reluctant. They worry the deja vu will be too much and emotions will flood back. Our open arms invite them to a familiar place in the journey. Events help strip away fear so they may join the community of grievers. We welcome them as we honor their pain.

Hospital memorial services gather families together to acknowledge the lives of tiny babies. Services can be yearly, quarterly or monthly. There may be a packed chapel or one lone family sitting in the second row, yet the message is the same: we celebrate the spirit of your baby and family. Holidays, especially Christmas, can be a difficult time of year for grieving parents. What should have been a wonderful and joyous time is now dark and empty. Coming together in a service can give a family the opportunity to remember their baby through loving sights and sounds. Providing families with a Christmas ornament or other memento can create a cherished remembrance.

There are other creative ways to be with families as they continue collecting memories. Some hospitals have memorial gardens, others have memorial quilts. Many hospitals are sponsoring remembrance walks, such as Walk To Remember. These bring families together as they remember the past and hope for tomorrow.

For some families, the physical space of the hospital is a consistent reminder of the emptiness and pain. They may choose not to return. The essence of a hospital event should be a consistent and ever-present offering where families know they are welcome, a healing part of the experience if they choose.

When families need more

Some families have trouble traveling the long road of grief. For them, grief is one small piece of a huge puzzle, impossible to solve. Other life crises mix in. Before they know it, they are swirling in the vortex of confusion. Their grief becomes complicated and affects their daily lives and all their relationships. As we continue to walk alongside, we must encourage them to seek out professional support. For many, it takes a lot of courage to reach out to a professional for help. Our role as their companion is to help them see it's part of their unique journey to healing.

They continue to teach us

Each family leaves an indelible impression on our mission as caregivers. When we experience the back side of grief, it strengthens our ability to care for families in acute situations. Past families teach us about courage and fortitude, about adaptation and change. They show us that a powerful hospital experience does make a difference in the months and years ahead. Our continued relationships are like steppingstones, leading us to the next family. Our fire gains strength as we prepare to go on.

CHAPTER TEN

FINAL THOUGHTS: FINDING JOY

Marcia tells her companioning story...

People ask me how I can find joy in all the sorrow. The joy, for me, is in watching a family come together in celebration of a tiny spirit. Like colors blending on a canvas, an unbearable situation slowly transforms into a moment of loving beauty. To go from something that might not be valued into a life that must be embraced and shared—there's a feeling that can't really be described. Joy is as close as it comes.

As we were finishing the last chapter of this book, I met a family who reminded me of the utter joy bereavement care brings. I felt the surge of warmth, the tingling down my back, the flow of oxygen in my lungs. I was able to connect, to companion. I did not make the difference; I was part of the difference.

Karla was admitted, 17 weeks pregnant, with symptoms of kidney infection. At first, Karla and Chad thought the pregnancy was not in danger, but that bubble burst when she went into labor and delivered. Tiny Zane was born with a faint heartbeat and his little transparent hands moved as he was held by his mother. The attending nurse, busy with other patients, did her best to comfort them in their grief. She gave them private time but Karla and Chad weren't sure how to say hello to their little baby. He looked so fragile, so different than expected. The nurse had suggested they call family but they wondered how others would see him. They decided it was best to keep their goodbyes private and spent only a short while with Zane after his death.

I spent time with them the next morning listening: to their pregnancy story, the fear of coming to the hospital, the shock of seeing the baby between her legs, the emptiness that was left. I concentrated on their comfort—a warm blanket and pain medications for mom, a cup of coffee and shower for dad. I wanted my offer of compassion to seep in slowly. I wanted to approach Zane's life on their time.

I created a sacred place to embrace Zane's life. I prepared a quieter room for them, complete with a rocking chair and a bassinette just for the baby. When they seemed ready, I suggested they move to the more soothing space, away from the noise and confusion of the unit. I bathed and redressed Zane, this time in a pastel blue wrap just his size. I gave them a picture adorned in a handmade frame, showing off his peaceful face.

In the new room, they napped and had lunch. When Karla awoke, she asked for Zane, ready to see him with fresh eyes. A soft lullaby in the background, Zane's precious body, swaddled in a blue and white knit blanket, was laid in his mother's arms once again. She cried, "Isn't he the most precious thing you have ever seen?" It must have felt safe now to look at his tiny toes and touch his face.

Chad began asking questions about burial. Slowly his thoughts moved from what needs to be done to what was the best way to honor this tiny life. They weren't ready to make any decisions but were uneasy about not doing something. I offered some suggestions to help fill the void; they liked the idea of having a small service in the hospital chapel before going home. "Could we take Zane with us?"

they asked. Hours after delivery, they were not sure if anyone would want to see Zane. Now, they wanted to carry him with pride in the midst of family and friends.

Thirty people joined them in celebrating Zane's life. A feeling of warmth filled the room. The chaplain spoke of the pain of love and many cried. It had been ten short hours since Zane had come into this world and quietly left. He was held by many and loved by all.

In the end, all we have is memories and the peace in knowing that what was done was right for us. What a privilege it was to help this new family move toward that peace as they made decisions that honored the spirit of their baby. Was I essential to that process? I don't know. All I know is that I felt blessed being a part and watching the growth happen before my eyes. And my heart was filled at the end of the day. If that's not joy, what is?

Joy and bereavement? To some, that may be an oxymoron, a conflicting match of words. How can happiness be connected to something so devastating? If we say we "enjoy" taking care of bereavement patients, what would others think?

As caregivers, we need to find meaning in the work we do. There has to be something out there to keep us going, to revive our passion for another day. Maybe it is joy: the emotional high, the inner warmth, the realization that we are part of something positive.

Unexpected joy

Marcia wasn't thinking about personal motivation when she met Karla and Chad, but she was drawn to the moment. Watching family members tenderly pass Zane's tiny body around during the service sent an unimaginable feeling pulsing throughout her body.

She witnessed a tender, life-changing moment: parents, family and friends unconditionally loving their tiny baby together. It made the knots in her shoulders and aches in her feet temporarily subside. As she drove home, her heart lightened. She felt blessed to be a part of this family's healing.

The search for joy may be the hardest part of the caregiver journey. It may be so mysterious that we let it slip by as we get caught up in logistics of care. It may be a quiet smile, a thank you card, a lasting hug. It may be so subtle we almost miss it: her muscles relaxing during a backrub, his attention as you bathe his baby, a silent glance as they go out the door. We must look for hidden messages of thankfulness. As Marcia talked with Chad about burial arrangements, she saw strained lines disappear from his face as his words changed from obligation to affirmation. Marcia thought to herself: *This is something powerful, something life-changing. He is ready for this part of the journey.* She was a conduit in the process, but it was his natural progression that led to that place. As Chad received clarity and vision, Marcia felt her companioning click into place. When she looked back on the moment, she realized it brought her unexpected joy.

Finding the inner joy

What is joy? It is like a cool breeze on a hot day, a cup of water when you're thirsty, a warm blanket on a snowy night. It is *refreshing*. It is not the same as happiness; it is about an inner satisfaction that renews. Joy is the fire that flames from our compassionate embers. It warms our souls.

As caregivers, we hope we can make a difference. Our hope is like a tiny seed that will sprout into a vine if it is nurtured and tended. The joy that follows is the fruit of the vine—a luscious, juicy byproduct that feeds our passion and fuels us for more giving.

There will always be sorrow in the reality of our work. It isn't morbid that we are drawn to bereavement. Each of us has a quiet voice inside that encourages us to find our passion and develop it. There are many reasons why some colleagues don't feel as we do. Maybe they are called to another end of the hall. Like grieving families, we each design our own journey. The fire of passion flames differently for each one of us.

We encourage you to take your time as you seek joy. Look for elements that bring light and clarity in your care. Hold onto the moments that stir that tingly feeling in your chest. Treasure the thank you notes, embraces, tears on your scrubs. Let each be another steppingstone in the search for meaning. If grief work is the dense green of the valley, joy is the unbelievable view from the mountaintop. Ultimately, it is your choice to climb the slope and find joy in bereavement. It is an exhausting journey but worth every step.

On behalf of the many families in your care—the ones before and the ones to come—thank you for your willingness to enter the wilderness. Accept the joy they give with open arms and be filled.